# The Lord's Prayer
and
# The Prayers of Our Lord

# The Lord's Prayer
and
# The Prayers of Our Lord

*A Scriptural Exposition*
*By* E. F. MORISON, D.D.
Late Scholar of Lincoln College, Oxford, and Senior Kennicott Scholar in University of Oxford. Author of 'St. Basil and his Rule,' etc.

WIPF & STOCK · Eugene, Oregon

Wipf and Stock Publishers
199 W 8th Ave, Suite 3
Eugene, OR 97401

The Lord's Prayer and The Prayers of Our Lord
A Scriptural Exposition
By Morison, E. F.
Softcover ISBN-13: 978-1-7252-8985-7
Hardcover ISBN-13: 978-1-7252-8986-4
Publication date 10/29/2020
Previously published by
SPCK / Sheldon Press / IVP UK, 1917

This edition is a scanned facsimile of
the original edition published in 1917.

## Preface

*THE* quotations from Scripture in this volume are taken from the Revised Version, except in the case of the Apocrypha, where Dr. Charles' edition has been used.

The author is grateful for permission to reprint Chapter III from the *Expository Times* and Chapter XII from the *Expositor*.

# Contents

| CHAP. | | PAGE |
|---|---|---|
| I. | When ye Pray | 1 |
| II. | The Divine Fatherhood | 11 |
| III. | The Father in Heaven | 28 |
| IV. | The Father's Name | 37 |
| V. | The Kingdom of the Father | 48 |
| VI. | The Will of the Father | 76 |
| VII. | Our Daily Bread | 91 |
| VIII. | Forgiveness | 109 |
| IX. | Protection and Deliverance | 123 |
| X. | Thanksgiving | 137 |
| XI. | The Lord's Prayer in St. Luke | 141 |
| XII. | Enthusiasm in St. Matthew | 159 |
| XIII. | Illustrations from Jewish Sources | 171 |
| XIV. | Versions of the Lord's Prayer | 181 |
| XV. | The Prayers of Our Lord | 185 |
| | Index of References | 191 |
| | General Index | 197 |

CHAPTER I

# When ye Pray

*'Ye shall seek me, and shall find me, when ye shall search for me with all your heart.'*—Jer. xxix. 13.

*T HIS* little work is intended to be neither a text-book nor a devotional commentary, but has been written as a scriptural exposition, to assist, as far as may be, those who would 'pray with the understanding.' Thoughtful prayer is not a contradiction in terms, nor does meditation necessarily involve the suspension of our reasoning faculty. We need to keep our devotion informed if we are to make any real progress in the spiritual life. The Lord's Prayer has suffered from having been too often regarded as the artless prattle of a child to its heavenly Father. Perhaps it is because we are taught the prayer in our earliest years that we are inclined to leave it thus unconsidered, a relic of childhood, a form for repetition, rather than a living expression of our reasoned hope and faith.

One of the first commentators upon the prayer, Tertullian of Carthage, described it as an 'epitome of the whole Gospel.'[1] By this he did not mean, surely, that each man may

[1] 'Breviarium totius evangelii,' Tertullian, *De Oratione*, c. i.

# The Lord's Prayer

consider the Lord's Prayer, as he prays it, to be a convenient summary of his own particular outlook on life, but that the Gospel of Jesus Christ is 'briefly comprehended in' the prayer which He taught to His disciples. We would seek to discover, therefore, what the Gospel, which is nowadays investigated with such close and minute attention in the endeavour to reveal the historic Christ, the earthly figure of the Son of Man, has to tell us with regard to the meaning and implications of the Lord's Prayer.

The sayings of Christ, indeed, may be considered as our most valuable source for the interpretation of the Lord's Prayer. Moreover, we are still further assisted towards the understanding of that prayer by the fact that certain of the utterances of our Lord which have come down to us are themselves prayers. They are few in number, for although the Evangelists often tell us that our Lord prayed, that He lifted up His eyes to heaven, or that He spent the whole night alone in prayer, yet very little is recorded by them as to the actual wording of His prayers. We are able, however, from the few scattered verses which the Synoptists give us, taken in conjunction with the long prayer of intercession and the other shorter prayers of the Fourth Gospel, to perceive quite plainly that our Lord when He taught His disciples to pray was instructing them in the light of His

# When ye Pray

own experience and from His own practice. Thus, as will be shown in the course of this investigation, our Lord was accustomed to address His prayer to the heavenly Father, to make request that God would 'glorify' His 'name,' to praise and thank Him for the progress of the Kingdom, and to pray the words, 'Thy will be done'; while in His forty days of prayer and fasting He learned the lesson of the Divine will that man should seek his food from God, yet that he does not live 'by bread alone,' but requires forgiveness for his sins and protection from the power of evil.

Our Lord, it is to be noticed, more than once prefixes to His teaching on the subject of prayer the words, 'When ye pray,' or 'When thou prayest.'[1] It is obvious, therefore, that He presupposes the habit of prayer on the part of those who heard Him, not merely because the Baptist had taught his disciples to pray, but because prayer was an essential factor in the life of the Jewish people. The prayers of the Jews in our Lord's day might need correction, the lengthy devotions of the Pharisee, for example, might often be hypocritical or self-complacent, yet the fact remains that the Jewish religion was pre-eminently a religion of prayer. Moreover, to the Jew prayer was not only a recognised fact, but a matter of living interest.

[1] *Cf.* Matt. vi. 5–7, Mark xi. 24 f., Luke xi. 2.

# The Lord's Prayer

How ought men to pray ? was the question they asked of all their religious leaders. The reason for this was, doubtless, due in large degree to the fact that the prayers of the ordinary public worship were regarded as insufficient and as requiring to be supplemented by prayers of a more personal and individual character. Yet it is necessary to remember that there was a further reason for the existence of independent and, as we may say, unauthorised devotions. The prayers of the Temple liturgy or of the Synagogue were in many cases unsuited to the needs of busy people, who were not able to spend the time which was necessary for their recitation. Consequently it was the habit of individual Rabbis to draw up short summaries of prayer, 'fountain prayers,' as they were called, for their own use and for the convenience of their followers. Thus it is recorded that Rabbi Akiba gave the injunction, 'If prayer be free in a man's mouth let him pray the Eighteen (Benedictions); but if not, let him pray the Fountain of the Eighteen.'[1]

The Lord's Prayer, therefore, may be regarded as a similar epitome—not indeed of any one particular prayer, but of all prayer. It was never intended to exclude other prayers, to supersede public worship, or to discourage private devotion, but rather to express the

[1] Berakoth, iv. 3.

# When ye Pray

spirit in which all prayer, all converse of man with God, should be offered. Our Lord gave to His followers a pattern prayer, a test-prayer as well as a summary, when He commanded, 'After this manner, therefore, pray ye.'[1] The comprehensiveness of the Lord's Prayer has been a favourite theme with commentators, but perhaps it has never been better expressed than by Bishop Latimer: 'As the law of love is the sum and abridgment of the other laws, so this Prayer is the sum and abridgment of all other prayers. All other prayers are contained in this Prayer; yea, whatsoever mankind hath need of as to soul and body, that same is contained in this Prayer.'[2]

We have seen, then, how prayer was regarded by the Jews as a matter of such fundamental importance that they took pains to provide that even the busiest worker might find time to pray. We are not therefore unduly alarmed when we are told that the Lord's Prayer is, to a very large extent, Judaic in its form and language. Our Lord was born as a Jew, and, in His own words, came 'not to destroy, but to fulfil'[3] the Jewish religion. Thus we may naturally suppose that He would not entirely discard but rather adapt to His own uses the

---

[1] Matt. vi. 9.
[2] Bp. Latimer, *Sermons*, p. 327 (Parker Society's Publications).    [3] Matt. v. 17.

# The Lord's Prayer

devotional language of His fellow-countrymen. The more parallels that can be adduced, whether from the Old Testament and the Apocrypha, or from rabbinical literature, to the various clauses of the Lord's Prayer, the more we rejoice that true prayer has, apparently, had such a continuous history.

A word of caution, however, must here be given. The mere citation of parallels is liable to be misleading. The instances which are adduced may be isolated rarities rather than characteristic examples. Thus there is much to be found both in the Talmud and in the Jewish liturgy that is of a very different character from those passages which have become commonplaces for the illustration of the New Testament, and there are many sentiments expressed other than those which are quoted for their similarity to the teaching of the Gospel. Quotations from Jewish sources are valuable for exposition, not for purposes of controversy. When therefore all the available evidence has been brought together to prove that the Lord's Prayer is Jewish in expression and in many of its sentiments, we still have to ask on what principle it omits so much that is equally Jewish. Further, even if, in the last resort—in the event, for example, of the discovery of new documents—we should be compelled to grant that the prayer

# When ye Pray

already existed and was actually used in certain Jewish circles, yet it does not thereby follow that the customary Jewish phrases, when taught by our Lord, could not have a new and fuller meaning. In our own Church worship we know what it is to pray the old familiar prayers 'with special intention,' and any prayer which was prayed to the Father, as revealed by Christ, with a view to the coming of the Kingdom, as defined by Christ, could no longer be merely Jewish. Hence, we repeat once again, the teaching of Christ is the truest interpretation of the Lord's Prayer.

There is, indeed, no necessity to consider too seriously these conjectures of Jewish polemic, which are substantiated by little or no evidence. It is interesting to be informed that the Lord's Prayer was probably taken over by the early Christian Church from the followers of the Baptist or from the Chasidim, the devout quietists among the Jews of the day, but no proof whatever can be given of such assertions. On the other hand, when we remember that there is good authority, in the combined evidence of the Gospels of St. Matthew and St. Luke, for attributing the prayer to Christ Himself, and that, in addition, every single clause is in itself a summary of some central point in Christ's teaching, we are under no obligation to surrender the traditional belief

# The Lord's Prayer

of Christendom that in the Lord's Prayer we have the actual prayer which Christ gave to His disciples as a model for their prayers.

We may here inquire whether the Gospels have anything to tell us with regard to the circumstances under which the Lord's Prayer was spoken. The Gospel of St. Matthew, it is to be noticed, merely inserts the Prayer into a section of the Sermon on the Mount which deals with the general subject of prayer, while a warning is prefixed as to the use of 'vain repetitions'[1] such as were characteristic of heathen worship. The disciples were not to weary God by a senseless reiteration of their requests. We are reminded of the prophets of Baal on Mount Carmel, who in their contest with Elijah, the prophet of Jehovah, cried 'from morning even until noon, saying O Baal, hear us.'[2] St. Luke, however, gives a very different setting to the delivery of the Lord's Prayer, and it is highly probable that his account is more in accordance with facts, even though we do not admit a similar veracity to his abbreviated version of its contents. It may be that here, as in certain other cases, he manifests the accuracy which he claims for his history of the Gospel rather by narrating true incident than by recording the exact details of discourse. Thus he says, 'And it came to pass, as Jesus

[1] Matt. vi. 7.   [2] 1 Kings xviii. 26.

## When ye Pray

was praying in a certain place,[1] that when he ceased, one of his disciples said unto him, Lord, teach us to pray, even as John taught his disciples. And he said unto them, When ye pray, say—'[2]

There are two features in this account from St. Luke which point to its authenticity. First, there is the reference to the Baptist. It is quite natural to assume that John taught his disciples to pray as well as to fast, though there is, as we have already stated, no evidence which may justify us in supposing that Christ adopted or revised a prayer which was already in use by the Baptist and his followers. Again, the picture of the disciples coming to our Lord and finding Him praying, and then, inspired by His example, desiring Him to teach them to pray has all the appearance of true description.

Moreover, the fact that our Lord had just ceased from praying when the disciples came to Him with their request suggests the possibility that He gave them a pattern for their devotions which was directly founded upon His own prayers. It will be seen from the detailed discussion which now follows how each clause, with the obvious exception of the petition for

---

[1] The conjecture has been made that this was the Garden of Gethsemane. J. A. Robinson, in F. H. Chase's *The Lord's Prayer in the Early Church*. (Texts and Studies, I. iii. pp. 123–5.)   [2] Luke xi. 1 f.

## The Lord's Prayer

forgiveness, reflects the prayers and aspirations of our Lord Himself. Thus to the statement that the teaching of Christ is the truest exposition of the Lord's Prayer we may add that the first and most important source of information as to the meaning of the Master's exemplar must be the language of His own prayers.

CHAPTER II

## The Divine Fatherhood

*'The Spirit of adoption, whereby we cry, Abba, Father.'*—Rom. viii. 15.

*W*HEN our Lord told His disciples to direct their prayers to God as Father He was able to commend His precept by His own example. The Gospels tell us that it was ever His habit to seek God in prayer and to call upon Him as Father. If the mission of Christ was to declare to men the love of God, it was natural that in His prayers, no less than in His work and teaching, He should seek to 'manifest' the 'name'[1] of His loving Father.

It was, indeed, in direct relation to the subject of prayer that our Lord claimed His unique knowledge of the Father and announced His authority to reveal the Divine Fatherhood to His fellow-men. Thus the prayer, 'Jesus answered and said, I thank thee, O Father, Lord of heaven and earth, that thou didst hide these things from the wise and understanding, and didst reveal them unto babes: yea, Father, for so it was well-pleasing in thy sight,' is immediately followed by the declaration, 'All things have been delivered unto me of my Father:

[1] John xvii. 6.

# The Lord's Prayer

and no one knoweth the Son, save the Father; neither doth any know the Father, save the Son, and he to whomsoever the Son willeth to reveal him.'[1]

In speaking of God, Jesus was wont to use various titles, but none so often as the simple name 'Father.' It is, of course, a commonplace that both the first and last words of our Saviour have direct reference to His heavenly Father, yet it is necessary to remember that the whole of our Lord's life here upon earth was a convincing witness to the Fatherhood of God. The boy Jesus, who at the early age of twelve already yearns to be busied about the things of the Father, grows into the man who in all things consults and obeys even unto death the will of the Divine Father.

We may here ask, how far was our Lord's insistence on the Fatherhood of God, more especially in its relation to prayer, original? Was the idea of addressing prayers to God as Father entirely unknown to those among whom Christ worked and taught? It has already been stated that to the Jew prayer was a familiar fact, and that our Lord when He gave His directions as to prayer evidently presupposed by His words, 'When ye pray,' that His hearers were in the habit of praying. Question, however, would still arise as to the proper form and method of prayer.

[1] Matt. xi. 25–7, Luke x. 21 f.

# The Divine Fatherhood

'Lord, teach us to pray,' was the request of the disciples. Are we then to suppose that our Lord, when He gave His instructions to His followers that they should approach God in prayer as the Divine Father, surprised them by the novelty of His doctrine?

There can be no doubt that here as elsewhere the teaching of Christ is founded upon Old Testament ideas. The Law and the Prophets had both spoken of God as Father, even though they did not order that He should be addressed by that title in prayer. The writings of the Prophets, more especially, contain clear intimations of the doctrine of the Fatherhood of God. 'When Israel was a child, then I loved him, and called my son out of Egypt,' is the word of the Lord in the prophet Hosea.[1] Again, in later days we have the striking pronouncement, 'For thou art our father, though Abraham knoweth us not, and Israel doth not acknowledge us; thou, O Lord, art our father; our redeemer from everlasting is thy name.'[2]

In spite, however, of these and other kindred passages, we are not a little disappointed that the idea of the Divine Fatherhood is given such slight prominence in the writings of the Old Testament. We might have expected that in the deep personal devotion of the Psalms, for example, we should have some clearer indication

---
[1] Hos. xi. 1.   [2] Isa. lxiii. 16.

# The Lord's Prayer

of God as the loving Father of all mankind. Yet the only reference to be found is the simile of Psalm ciii., 'Like as a father pitieth his children, so the Lord pitieth them that fear him,'[1] and the assertion, 'A father of the fatherless, and a judge of the widows, is God in his holy habitation.'[2]

This representation of God as Father is not only wanting in emphasis, it is exceedingly narrow in its application. Even though Jehovah may be spoken of as in some sense the Father of the Jewish nation, He is not recognised as the Father of all mankind. The Jew may indeed say, 'Have we not all one father ? hath not one God created us ?'[3] yet Jehovah is not yet declared to be the universal Father who loves and cares for each one of His children.

Further, this special relation of God to the chosen people which is involved in the Old Testament idea of Jehovah as the Father of the nation is as little personal in character as it is universal in extent. The Jewish nation, or the Messiah as the national representative, is the object of God's care. 'I will establish the throne of his kingdom for ever. I will be his father, and he shall be my son.'[4]

If God, then, was so seldom and in so limited a sense thought of as Father, we cannot wonder

[1] Ps. ciii. 13.  
[2] Ps. lxviii. 5.  
[3] Mal. ii. 10.  
[4] 2 Sam. vii. 14.

## The Divine Fatherhood

that prayer was not addressed to Him under that title. As a matter of fact, we find that in the Old Testament prayers are directed to Jehovah as 'the Lord God,'[1] 'the Lord of hosts,'[2] 'the God of Israel,'[3] 'the great and dreadful God,'[4] 'the God of heaven, the great and terrible God.'[5] The God of the Jews was to be supplicated with fear and trembling by His worshippers.

Yet this is not always the case. In the Prophets and the Psalms there are prayers in which Jehovah is approached with confidence and love. In the Book of Jeremiah, for example, the Lord is entreated as 'Thou hope of Israel, the saviour thereof in the time of trouble.'[6] Again, there is the prayer in the Book of Isaiah which we have already quoted as being addressed to God as 'Father.'[7] Here too He is spoken of as 'their saviour.'[8] In the Psalter, whether we regard the Psalms as individual or national in their origin and expression, we find that God is prayed to under such titles as 'Thou that savest them which put their trust in thee,'[9] 'the God of my

---

[1] Gen. xv. 2.
[2] 2 Sam. vii. 27.
[3] *Ibid.*, 1 Kings viii. 25.
[4] Dan. ix. 4.
[5] Neh. i. 5, ix. 32 ; *cf.* Deut. vii. 21.
[6] Jer. xiv. 8.
[7] Isa. lxiii. 16 ; *cf.* lxiv. 8.
[8] Isa. lxiii. 8.
[9] Ps. xvii. 7.

# The Lord's Prayer

salvation,'[1] 'the Shepherd of Israel,'[2] or 'the Lord my Rock.'[3]

The Apocrypha, as is well known, attaches the highest importance to prayer. Thus Tobit in his advice to his son says, 'Bless the Lord thy God at all times, and ask of him that thy ways may be made straight, and that all thy paths and counsels may prosper.'[4] So too Raphael declares 'Good is prayer with fasting and alms and righteousness.'[5] In the Book of Wisdom also it is enjoined, 'We must rise before the sun to give thee thanks, and must plead with thee at the dawning of the light.'[6] Do we then find that in the many prayers which the Apocrypha contains God is addressed as Father? The title is occasionally used, but it is by no means frequent, and its significance is somewhat vague. There is a prayer in the Book of Ecclesiasticus in which the following invocation is to be found: 'O Lord, Father and Master of my life,'[7] but the idea conveyed seems to be that of guidance and control rather than of loving care. So also in the Book of Wisdom, in the account of a ship at sea, we read: 'Thy providence, O Father, guideth it along.'[8]

[1] Ps. lxxxviii. 1.
[2] Ps. lxxx. 1.
[3] Ps. xxviii. 1.
[4] Tobit iv. 19.
[5] Tobit xii. 8.
[6] Wisd. xvi. 28.
[7] Ecclus. xxiii. 1.
[8] Wisd. xiv. 3.

# The Divine Fatherhood

A certain development, however, may be observed in this idea of the Fatherhood of God. We can see that the belief in a Divine Father is becoming more personal, more individual in character. Thus, to quote again from the Book of Wisdom, the righteous man is upbraided by his enemies because 'he vaunteth that God is his father,'[1] and after his death the question is asked, 'How was he numbered among sons of God, and how is his lot among saints?'[2] In the thanksgiving of Tobit we have the express declaration, 'He is our Lord, and he our God, and he our Father.'[3] So also in the Book of Jubilees (c. 120 B.C.), 'They all shall be called children of the living God, and every angel and every spirit shall know, yea, they shall know that these are my children, and that I am their Father in uprightness and righteousness, and that I love them.'[4]

It is quite likely that amongst the Rabbis of our Lord's own day the title 'Father in heaven' was employed as a name for God. Yet the idea of God as the universal Father had entered very little into the popular consciousness, the legal idea of God as Ruler and King being still the dominant one. The religion of Judaism failed because it was unable to complement the kingly power of the Almighty with

[1] Wisd. ii. 16.     [2] Wisd. v. 5.
[3] Tobit xiii. 4.     [4] Jub. i. 25.

# The Lord's Prayer

the kindly love of God as the Father of all. Further, the Jew still regarded the Divine Fatherhood as a matter of national privilege. Thus St. Paul reckons amongst the glories of the Jewish race 'the adoption.'[1] Yet St. Paul fully realised that what was needed for his fellow-countrymen was not a proud boastfulness in the exclusive possession of such 'legal sonship,' but rather the humble 'spirit of adoption,' the love of the child, who can 'cry, Abba, Father.'[2]

Our Lord, as has often been observed, was in the habit of giving new emphasis and meaning to the religious terms current in His day. It is so with such expressions as 'the Kingdom of Heaven,' or 'the Son of Man,' and it is more especially the case with the title 'Father,' as applied by Him to God. Here His use of a conventional term amounts almost to a new revelation. Not only is the name Father employed with greater frequency and more pointed emphasis, but its meaning is immeasurably fuller. Instead of being a mere occasional title, it is used by Jesus as His habitual name for God. The whole teaching, indeed, of Jesus may be regarded as an interpretation of the one great central fact, the Fatherhood of God, 'my Father and your Father.'[3]

---

[1] Rom. ix. 4.  [2] Rom. viii. 15.
[3] John xx. 17.

# The Divine Fatherhood

It is only possible here to give a very brief outline of our Lord's actual use of the word Father as a name for God. We have already noted that He claimed to have absolute and unique knowledge as to the Divine Fatherhood, that His first and last recorded utterances both have reference to His heavenly Father, and that in His prayers He was wont to call upon God as Father. There is here no abstraction or euphemism such as the Jews of our Lord's day were accustomed to employ in speaking of the Divinity, but a direct personal appeal to the God of Love Himself. The Christ would teach us that the relation of the suppliant to God is best illustrated and explained by the simple facts of family life. 'If ye then, being evil, know how to give good gifts unto your children, how much more shall your Father which is in heaven give good things to them that ask him?'[1] And this is to be done not merely because He is 'my Father,' but because He is 'your Father which is in heaven.' 'The Father himself loveth you.'[2]

We should notice that God is spoken of and addressed as Father, not merely because He is Creator, or because He is the All-Ruler, but rather because He is Love. The Christian Creed proclaims our faith in 'God Almighty, Maker of heaven and earth,' but it has always declared

[1] Matt. vii. 11.    [2] John xvi. 27.

## The Lord's Prayer

also our belief in a loving Father, as revealed by Jesus Christ,—' I believe in God *the Father.*' For the Fatherhood of God is a fact of supreme significance. The Son of Man is the impersonation of entire humanity and He tells us that His Divine Father cares for each one of us. By our following of Christ we may become children of God. Thus our Lord when He bids us love our enemies adds 'that ye may be sons of your Father which is in heaven.'[1] We are also bidden in the same command to realise the brotherhood of man, for the heavenly Father 'maketh his sun to rise on the evil and the good, and sendeth rain on the just and the unjust.'[2]

The Divine Fatherhood is not manifested merely towards avowed disciples, though, naturally, there must be a response to His gracious favours. The devout follower is himself to be a witness to the world at large of the Father's love. Hence it is that our Lord says to His disciples, 'Let your light shine before men, that they may see your good works, and glorify your Father which is in heaven.'[3] The Divine love is both intensive and extensive, and the Kingdom of God grows and spreads until it reach fulfilment. 'Ye therefore shall be perfect, as your heavenly Father is perfect.'[4]

[1] Matt. v. 45.
[2] *Ibid.*
[3] Matt. v. 16.
[4] Matt. v. 48.

# The Divine Fatherhood

We are indeed all members of one great family, the household of God. The heavenly Fatherhood is the one, perfect, and all-embracing Fatherhood; 'Call no man your father upon the earth: for one is your Father, which is in heaven.'[1]

Here, however, we need to be on our guard against a conception of God as mere beneficence, *le bon Dieu*. The love of the Father is essentially a personal and ethical relation. God is concerned with creation; He 'made and loveth all,' but mankind is the special and most intimate object of His love: He is 'the good God who loveth *us*.' The care of God for the animal world is only an evidence of His greater love for mankind. 'Are ye not much better than they, yet your heavenly Father feedeth them.'[2]

Being a moral relationship, the love of God must not be obscured by sin. Thus the Prodigal in the parable feels that by his sins he has forfeited his sonship, his place in the family of the Divine Father. 'I will arise and go to my father, and will say unto him, Father, I have sinned against heaven, and in thy sight: I am no more worthy to be called thy son.'[3] Sonship consists in a moral likeness to the Father which is destroyed by sin. 'God is love,'[4] but at the same time 'none is good save one,

[1] Matt. xxiii. 9.  [2] Matt. vi. 26.
[3] Luke xv. 18.  [4] 1 John iv. 8.

# The Lord's Prayer

even God.'[1] Thus the 'Our Father' may well serve as the prayer of the penitent who 'comes to himself,'[2] and would renew the loving relationship which sin has spoiled.

'The spirit of adoption,' then, is the outpouring of love, expressed in the simple word 'Father,' which our Lord has taught us to pray. 'Father of all, to Thee with loving hearts we pray' are words which breathe the true spirit of all sincere and spontaneous prayer. For indeed the true 'Lord's Prayer' is not the reiterated *Paternoster*, but the natural utterance of those who as 'little children' would 'enter into the kingdom of heaven.'[3]

It remains for us now to consider the actual manner in which our Lord addressed His own prayers to His Father, for as He was the Son of Man, not only the prayer which He ordered, but the prayers which He Himself used, are the models for humanity. We are often told, possibly with too great emphasis, that the 'Our Father' was prescribed for the disciple, but was not used by the Master himself. Yet, as we shall see, the prayers of our Lord were prayed in the same spirit and often in the same words as that which we call 'the Lord's Prayer.'

The first prayer of Christ of which the words are recorded is the prayer of thanksgiving which,

[1] Matt. xix. 17 (R.V. marg.).     [2] Luke xv. 17.
[3] Matt. xviii. 3.

## The Divine Fatherhood

St. Luke tells us, was occasioned by the return of the Seventy from their mission in Galilee. 'I thank thee, O Father, Lord of heaven and earth, that thou didst hide these things from the wise and understanding, and didst reveal them unto babes: yea, Father; for so it was well pleasing in thy sight.'[1] Here we notice first the act of loving thankfulness, the prayer of gratitude for the results of the preaching of the kingdom of heaven. The prayer is addressed to the 'Father, Lord of heaven and earth,' who is both the loving Father and the Ruler of the universe, who so ordereth all things that the 'foolishness of God is wiser than men; and the weakness of God is stronger than men.'[2]

In the Agony of Gethsemane our Lord, we are told, prayed the same words three times, 'Abba, Father, all things are possible unto thee; remove this cup from me: howbeit not what I will, but what thou wilt.'[3] The words of invocation in this prayer are given variously by the three Evangelists as 'Abba, Father,'[4] 'O my Father,'[5] or simply 'Father.'[6] The prayer is addressed not so much to the Almighty Ruler, the Supreme Disposer,—though St. Mark records the words, 'all things are possible unto thee,'[7]—

---

[1] Luke x. 21, Matt. xi. 25 f.
[2] 1 Cor. i. 25.
[3] Mark xiv. 36.
[4] *Ibid.*
[5] Matt. xxvi. 42.
[6] Luke xxii. 42.
[7] Mark xiv. 36.

# The Lord's Prayer

as to the Father who loves and supports His Son in this hour of trial. This offering up of 'prayers and supplications with strong crying and tears unto him that was able to save him from death,'[1] was, in spite of its tragic sorrow, a testimony of His loving intimacy with the heavenly Father from which no shame or suffering at human hands could separate Him.

Again, in the Words from the Cross the Saviour directs His prayers to His heavenly Father. It is to the Father of all mankind that He prays for His enemies, 'Father, forgive them; for they know not what they do.'[2] He thus fulfils His own precept, 'Love your enemies, and pray for them that persecute you, that ye may be sons of your Father which is in heaven.'[3] In His last words, His prayer of resignation, it is to His Father's keeping that He commends His spirit. Though in the desolation of His sorrow He had quoted the words of the Psalmist, 'My God, my God, why hast thou forsaken me?'[4] and had made no demands upon the Divine Fatherhood, yet when in His last earthly utterance He again uses words from the Psalms we take notice that to the accustomed phrase, 'Into thy hands I commend my spirit,' He adds the loving invocation, the supreme title of trust and confidence, 'Father.'[5]

[1] Heb. v. 7.
[2] Luke xxiii. 34.
[3] Matt. v. 44.
[4] Mark xv. 34, Matt. xxvii. 46.
[5] Luke xxiii. 46.

## The Divine Fatherhood

In the Fourth Gospel, at the end of the discourses spoken by our Lord at the Last Supper, we have given us a long prayer in which our Lord prays His Father to 'glorify' Him, and to keep and protect His disciples. The great crisis is at hand, and Jesus prays for strength and guidance for Himself and for His followers. The prayer, which is part supplication and part thanksgiving, is directly addressed to the heavenly Father, 'These things spake Jesus; and lifting up his eyes to heaven, he said, Father, the hour is come; glorify thy Son, that the Son may glorify thee.'[1] In the course of the prayer the Father is several times invoked, four times as 'Father,'[2] once as 'Holy Father,'[3] and once as 'O righteous Father.'[4] The words of this prayer are the expression of ardent love, love for His Father and love for His brethren whom he consigns to His Father's keeping. 'Holy Father, keep them in thy name which thou hast given me, that they may be one, even as we are.'[5]

On a previous occasion, when Andrew and Peter brought certain Greeks to Jesus, we read that our Lord prayed a similar prayer, 'Father, glorify thy name.'[6] Here, however, the element of thanksgiving is absent. The dark tragedy is but just beginning. 'Now is my soul troubled;

[1] John xvii. 1.    [2] John xvii. 1, 5, 21, 24.
[3] John xvii. 11.    [4] John xvii. 25.
[5] John xvii. 11.    [6] John xii. 28.

# The Lord's Prayer

and what shall I say? Father, save me from this hour. But for this cause came I unto this hour.'[1] Here once again our Lord prays that His sacred mission to reveal the name, the Fatherhood, of God to all mankind may be fulfilled, and that so the name of the Father may be glorified in the Son. The 'voice from heaven' which comes in answer to the prayer declares, 'I have both glorified it, and will glorify it again.'[2] The sign of the heavenly voice is given, we are told, not to assure the Christ that His prayers are answered, but to convince His followers. 'This voice hath not come for my sake, but for your sakes.'[3]

The same regard for His disciples and His audience is manifested in another prayer recorded in the Fourth Gospel, at the raising of Lazarus. 'And Jesus lifted up his eyes, and said, Father, I thank thee that thou heardest me. And I knew that thou hearest me always: but because of the multitude which standeth around I said it, that they may believe that thou didst send me.'[4] The prayers of our Lord were not always said in private or on the mountain-top. But whether said privately or in the hearing of others, they seem always to have been directed to God as Father.

In concluding this subject we may say that,

[1] John xii. 27.  [2] John xii. 28.
[3] John xii. 30.  [4] John xi. 41 f.

# The Divine Fatherhood

as we read the Gospel story, we see plainly that for our Lord prayer was a continuous communion with His loving Father. He told His followers to pray to God as Father, because prayer to the Father was the inspiration, the joy, and the comfort of His whole life. 'These things I speak in the world, that they might have my joy fulfilled in themselves.'[1]

[1] John xvii. 13.

CHAPTER III

# The Father in Heaven

'*Our Father which art in heaven.*'—Matt. vi. 9.
'*One God and Father of all, who is over all, and through all, and in all.*'—Eph. iv. 6.

*I*N the two versions of the Lord's Prayer which are given to us in the Gospels there is considerable divergence in the words of the invocation, or address to God, and there has consequently been much discussion as to which of the two forms 'Father,'[1] or 'Our Father which art in heaven,'[2] is the more authentic.

Liturgical usage has always preferred the longer form, but we are here concerned not with the history of the Lord's Prayer in the worship of the Church so much as with the actual wording, if we may discover it, of the prayer as taught by Christ to His disciples in response to their request, 'Lord, teach us to pray.'[3] The question, perhaps, is not one of fundamental importance, and we may feel that it is enough for us to know that, in any case, the Master bade His followers address the God to whom they prayed as 'Father.'[3]

At the same time it is worth while for us

[1] Luke xi. 2.   [2] Matt. vi. 9.
[3] Luke xi. 1.

## The Father in Heaven

to remember that there is another prayer in the Gospels, the prayer of our Lord in the Garden of Gethsemane, where similar variations are to be found in the form of the invocation. Thus, as we have already noticed, while St. Luke begins the prayer of the Agony with the simple address, 'Father,'[1] St. Matthew gives the words 'O my Father.'[2] It is also noteworthy that St. Mark in his version of this same prayer has the invocation in the Pauline form, 'Abba, Father.'[3] Hence it would seem highly probable that the Lord's Prayer originally began with the single word of address, 'Abba,' which was rendered by St. Luke as 'Father,' and by St. Matthew as 'Our Father,' both being legitimate renderings of the Aramaic term.

How, then, are we to explain the expression 'Abba, Father,' as employed both by St. Mark and St. Paul? It has often been suggested that the phrase is a liturgical formula and represents the usage of the earliest Christians in their public worship. Our Lord Himself is not likely to have used the expression, for there is no reason to suppose that, even if He spoke Aramaic and Greek, He would therefore employ bilingual phrases in His prayers to God. But it is more than probable that in

[1] Luke xxii. 42.  [2] Matt. xxvi. 42.
[3] Mark xiv. 36.

# The Lord's Prayer

communities of mixed race and speech such bilingual expressions, especially in a case of solemn invocation, would be used. Thus we may suppose that both St. Paul and St. Mark when they employ the words 'Abba, Father' reflect the liturgical usage of their day, the 'Common Prayer' of the primitive Church.

We may here remark that to suppose the original wording of the invocation to have been the simple 'Abba,' or 'Father,' in no way detracts from the social significance of the prayer. It was possible for a family, no less than for an individual, to say 'Abba.' The use also of the first person plural in the clauses 'give *us* this day *our* daily bread,' 'forgive *us our* trespasses,' and 'deliver *us* from the evil one,' strongly emphasises the corporate aspect of the prayer and its fitness for public as well as private recitation. 'Publica est nobis et communis oratio,' says St. Cyprian in his comments on the invocation.[1] 'The name Father loses its significance for us individually, when we will not use it as the members of a family,' remarks Maurice in his sermon on this subject.[2]

It is not easy to say with any degree of certainty why the phrase 'which art in heaven' occurs only in St. Matthew, and is not to be

[1] Cyprian, *De Oratione Dominica*, viii.
[2] F. D. Maurice, *The Lord's Prayer*, I. ii.

## The Father in Heaven

found in the shorter form of the Lord's Prayer which is recorded by St. Luke. In any case there is no reason to conclude that the shorter version is of necessity the truer, for *brevius verius* has never been propounded as an axiom of criticism. We may, of course, maintain, as Origen and many subsequent commentators have done, that the Lord's Prayer was given twice, the longer form first to the disciples as a body and the shorter form later in answer to the request of a single disciple. Or we may even imagine that the shorter form was given first, and that the longer version was delivered later as the result of further reflection. Thus a recent writer on the Gospels has said, 'Admitting that Matthew's version is later than and an amplification of Luke's, we are still not precluded from supposing that Matthew's, too, may have proceeded from Jesus Himself,'[1] and he intimates that our Lord may have had good reasons for further concentrating the attention of His disciples upon the invisible, spiritual kingdom, the dwelling-place of the heavenly Father.

On the other hand, if we suppose, as is, perhaps, more natural, that the pattern prayer of our Lord originally existed in only one form, as having been actually delivered in that form alone, we cannot there-

[1] E. A. Abbott, *The Son of Man*, p. 601.

# The Lord's Prayer

fore take for granted that the phrase 'which art in heaven' is an insertion, an addition made by some early Jewish-Christian disciple to the original title of address. It is more probable, as we shall seek to prove later, that the words were intentionally omitted by St. Luke from his version of the Lord's Prayer, in order to avoid the danger, in preaching to the Gentile world, of localising the Deity in heaven, as distinguished from earth. There are many signs in his Gospel that for St. Luke heaven was the abode of the angels rather than the throne of God, the 'Lord of heaven *and* earth.'[1]

Whatever may be said as to the origin of the phrase 'which art in heaven' in the invocation of the Lord's Prayer, there is certainly, it must be allowed, some considerable evidence in favour of these words when we consider the language which our Lord is recorded to have used in His own prayers. Thus His Prayer of Thanksgiving, according to both St. Matthew and St. Luke, begins with the words, 'I thank thee, O Father, Lord of heaven and earth,'[2] and not merely with the simple invocation, 'Father.' Furthermore, we are told in the Fourth Gospel that Jesus when He prayed 'lifted up his eyes to heaven,'[3] and that when He performed

---

[1] Matt. xi. 25, Luke x. 21.
[2] *Ibid.*
[3] John xvii. 1; *cf.* xi. 41.

## The Father in Heaven

miracles He 'looked up to heaven.'[1] So also the 'voice from heaven' which was heard at His Baptism, at the Transfiguration, and, according to the Fourth Gospel, at the coming of the Greeks to Jesus, seems to have been given in answer to the prayers of our Lord.[2] Lastly, in the Lord's Prayer itself, in St. Matthew's version, there is the clause 'as in heaven, so on earth,'[3] which occurs quite naturally in a prayer addressed to the Father who is 'in heaven,' so that we may suppose these two phrases to be closely connected, and that what is evidence for the one is evidence for the other.

In the writings of the Old Testament it can be plainly seen that there is much to justify such an invocation of God as is expressed in the words 'which art in heaven.' Jehovah is repeatedly spoken of or invoked by the title 'maker,' or 'possessor of heaven and earth,'[4] or, more simply, as 'the God of heaven and earth,' or 'the God of heaven.'[5] It is from heaven that He hears the prayers of His suppliant people, 'Hear thou in heaven thy dwelling-place; and when thou hearest, forgive.' Further, in the rabbinical literature the term 'Father in heaven' occurs with some frequency.

---

[1] Matt. xiv. 19, Mark vi. 41, vii. 34, Luke ix. 16.
[2] John xii. 28.  [3] Matt. vi. 10.
[4] Gen. xiv. 19, 22; *cf.* Isa. li. 13, Ps. cxlvi. 6, etc.
[5] Neh. i. 4, Dan. ii. 19, etc.

## The Lord's Prayer

Thus in reply to the question 'Upon whom shall we lean?' the answer is given, 'Upon our Father who is in heaven,'[1] and we find the exhortation, 'Be bold as a leopard, and light as an eagle, and swift as a gazelle, and strong as a lion to do the will of thy Father which is in heaven.'[2]

The actual meaning of the words 'which art in heaven' is plain enough. They have a real significance in this pattern prayer. They bid us consider, as we make our supplications, the majesty of Him to whom we pray, 'the high and lofty One that inhabiteth eternity, whose name is Holy.'[3] Thus, in directing his prayers to the heavenly Father, the disciple follows the example of the Master in 'lifting up his eyes to heaven.'[4] The title of address expresses the reverence of the worshipper, not the remoteness of God. The thought is not 'God is in heaven, and thou upon earth: therefore let thy words be few,'[5] but rather, 'Whom have I in heaven but thee? And there is none upon earth that I desire beside thee.'[6] We can therefore draw near to the Father in full confidence, for, as our Lord Himself has told us, 'Your heavenly Father knoweth that ye have need of all these things,'[7] and 'the Father himself loveth you.'[8]

[1] Sotah ix. 11.
[2] Pirke Aboth, v. 23.
[3] Isa. lvii. 15.
[4] John xvii. 1, etc.
[5] Eccles. v. 2.
[6] Ps. lxxiii. 25
[7] Matt. vi. 32.
[8] John xvi. 27.

## The Father in Heaven

Again, inasmuch as He is our Father in heaven, He is powerful to save those whom He loves. As our Lord Himself prayed, so also we pray, 'All things are possible unto thee.'[1] Though our earthly fathers fail us, yet 'the Lord is nigh unto all them that call upon him.'[2] 'One is your Father, the heavenly.'[3] He is omnipotent for our salvation, and to Him we ascribe 'the kingdom, *the power*, and the glory, for ever and ever, Amen.'

And so we are not afraid to approach Him, though He be 'high and lifted up,'[4] for as children of the one family we may 'draw near with a true heart in full assurance of faith.'[5] Dr. Gore, in his comment on these words of invocation, has well remarked: 'We call Him the *Father which is in heaven*, not because He is far off from us—for in the Kingdom of Christ heavenly and earthly things are mingled and we "are come unto the heavenly Jerusalem,"[6] but because He is raised far above all the pollution and wilfulness and ignorance of man "as the heaven is higher than the earth."[7] So we invoke our Father, infinitely above us yet unspeakably near.'[8]

In conclusion, therefore, it may be said that,

[1] Mark xiv. 36.  [2] Ps. cxlv. 18.
[3] Matt. xxiii. 9 (R.V. marg.).
[4] Isa. vi. 1.  [5] Heb. x. 22.
[6] Heb. xii. 22.  [7] Isa. lv. 9.
[8] Gore, *The Sermon on the Mount*, p. 122.

# The Lord's Prayer

though in the form of the Lord's Prayer which St. Luke gives us the one simple word 'Father' stands impressively alone, yet the fuller, and probably more authentic,[1] version of the address which we find in St. Matthew is of the utmost value for the whole thought and meaning of the Prayer, as expressing our reverent faith in the Father of all, who will with His heavenly power help and guide His children upon earth.

[1] Dr. Chase calls attention to Mark xi. 25, ' And whensoever ye stand praying, forgive, if ye have ought against anyone; that your Father also which is in heaven may forgive you your trespasses.' He says, ' It is the only passage in St. Mark in which this name of God, *the Father in Heaven, the Heavenly Father*, is found; and consequently its witness is strongly in favour of the form ὁ ἐν τοῖς οὐρανοῖς being the current Greek form of the first clause of the Lord's Prayer.' F. H. Chase, *The Lord's Prayer in the Early Church*, p. 22 f.

CHAPTER IV

# The Father's Name

*'Hallowed be thy name.'*—Matt. vi. 9.
*'Glorify thy name.'*—John xii. 28.

*IN* any investigation of this first petition of the Lord's Prayer we have no need to perplex ourselves with questions of textual criticism, for both Matthew and Luke record the words in a precisely identical form. Further, we may also allow that in regard to its interpretation there is no reason why this petition should not be the first of those which we address to God, for just as in the invocation we call upon God by His Name ' Father,' so here we pray that the Divine Name, as thus revealed, may everywhere be sanctified, recognised as holy.

The connection, however, between the title of the invocation and the meaning of this clause has, perhaps, not always been sufficiently realised by expositors of the Lord's Prayer. It is true, no doubt, that the expression ' Let thy name be hallowed ' has a general significance, that it is a prayer for the growth and spread of true religion : ' the fear of the Lord is the beginning of wisdom,'[1] and ' unto you that fear my name shall the sun of righteousness arise.'[2] In this

[1] Prov. ix. 10.  [2] Mal. iv. 2.

## The Lord's Prayer

same sense also we may say that the first petition of the Lord's Prayer is a true 'Missionary Prayer,' a prayer for the expansion of the knowledge of the Lord, as is further exemplified by the language of the Apocalypse, 'Who shall not fear, O Lord, and glorify thy name? for thou only art holy; for all the nations shall come and worship before thee; for thy righteous acts have been made manifest.'[1]

Yet we may surely see a more particular meaning in this prayer for the sanctification of the Divine Name. The expression, of course, has its roots in the past, is illustrated by prophet, lawgiver, and psalmist, but in the model prayer for the followers of Christ it has also a further implication: 'May Thy Name Father be hallowed and revered by those who must become as little children before they can enter the kingdom of Heaven.' The simple and spontaneous address 'Father' of the invocation may indeed be said to influence every word of the prayer thus directed to Him. 'They that know thy name,' says the Psalmist, 'will put their trust in thee,'[2] and those who call upon God as Father and have a true faith in His fatherly love may well pray that this one, great, and all-important fact of the Fatherhood of God may be realised, that all the implications of the supreme revelation, the name *Father*, may come to be fully

[1] Rev. xv. 4.   [2] Ps. ix. 10.

## The Father's Name

recognised by the whole human race. There is thus something deeper, more personal and more vital, in such a prayer than a mere pious aspiration for the furtherance of religion. It is not a conventional liturgical formula, as in the Jewish petition, 'Let His great Name be blessed for ever, and to all eternity,'[1] but the expression of a deep yearning that each and all of God's children may find their true home 'in the kingdom of their Father.'[2]

It would, perhaps, be difficult to find a more familiar Jewish term than the expression 'the Name of the Lord.' In the Decalogue the command is given, 'Thou shalt not take the name of the Lord thy God in vain,'[3] and in the Levitical Code speaking against God is described as 'blaspheming the name.'[4] Further, the House of God is described in Deuteronomy as 'the place which the Lord shall choose to cause his name to dwell there.'[5] In the prophecies of Ezekiel we read: 'And I will sanctify my great name, which hath been profaned among the nations, which ye have profaned in the midst of them; and the nations shall know that I am the Lord, saith the Lord God, when I shall be sanctified in you before their eyes.'[6] It cannot be said that there is not good authority in the

---
[1] *Cf.* Singer, *Authorised Daily Prayer Book*, p. 37.
[2] Matt. xiii. 43.   [3] Exod. xx. 7.   [4] Lev. xxiv. 11.
[5] Deut. xii. 11, etc.        [6] Ezek. xxxvi. 23.

# The Lord's Prayer

scriptures of the Old Testament for the 'hallowing' of the Divine Name.

Our Lord Jesus Christ, however, gives a plainer meaning and a more definite content to the expression, 'the name of the Lord.' It is no longer an equivalent for the gradual and partial revelation of the character of God, whether to the Gentiles amongst whom He 'left not himself without witness,'[1] nor even to the Jews to whom He was known as 'Jehovah, the God of Israel.'[2] For Jesus the Divine Name is simply 'Father,' and it is for the hallowing of that name, in some sense 'a new name,'[3] that He bids His disciples pray. We do not, if we pray in the spirit of Christ, address our prayers to Jehovah, 'the glorious and fearful name,'[4] nor do we pray that the nations of the world may praise His 'great and terrible name: holy is he,'[5] but rather we make petition to our heavenly Father that 'thy way may be known upon earth, thy saving health among all nations.'[6]

It may seem strange that in the life and words of our Lord as recorded by the first three Evangelists there should be no further mention of the hallowing of 'the name.' Other clauses of the Lord's Prayer have their counterpart in sayings

[1] Acts xiv. 17.
[2] Exod. xxxii. 27, etc.
[3] Rev. ii. 17.
[4] Deut. xxviii. 58.
[5] Ps. xcix. 3.
[6] Ps. lxvii. 2.

## The Father's Name

of our Lord spoken on other occasions, but in this case, apparently, there is no exact parallel to be found in these Gospels to this prayer for the sanctification, the devout recognition of the Divine Name *Father*. Possibly this is due to the fact that our Lord deliberately refused to employ the expression 'the Name' as a periphrasis for God, and chose to speak of Him directly as 'Father,' 'my Father,' or 'your Father.' The phrase, therefore, has here a special significance as employing a term which in itself was not customary to our Lord. At the same time, however, a prayer which was definitely and immediately addressed to God as Father could safely and rightly include a petition for the worship of His holy Name, a fervent prayer that others may come to join their prayers with those who call upon God as the Father of all. The Lord's Prayer is the great 'family prayer.' We are bidden to pray for the advent of the Kingdom, for the fulfilment of the Divine Will, but first and foremost, as including all else, we pray that the whole family of mankind may be led to realise their birthright, 'the right to become children of God.'[1]

On the other hand, when we turn to the Gospel according to St. John, we find that 'the name' of God is repeatedly mentioned, and there is much that serves to illustrate

[1] John i. 12.

# The Lord's Prayer

our Lord's use of the expression, 'May thy name be hallowed,' in His pattern prayer. We have already remarked that the clause is no mere liturgical formula, or an ascription of praise inserted in accordance with the rabbinic principle, 'A benediction that does not mention the Name is no benediction at all.'[1] It must be noticed, however, that although in the Fourth Gospel the Name of God is not infrequently spoken of, yet it is always in a direct personal relation, 'thy name,' or else with immediate reference to the Divine Fatherhood, 'the name of the Father,' or 'of my Father.' The prayer of our Lord which is given in chapter xvii. of the Gospel makes mention of the Name of the Father no less than four times. 'I manifested thy name unto the men whom thou gavest me out of the world.'[2] 'Holy Father, keep them in thy name which thou hast given me.'[3] 'While I was with them, I kept them in thy name which thou hast given me.'[4] 'I made known unto them thy name, and will make it known.'[5] These passages make it clear that here, at any rate, the 'name' of God is not a vague generalisation, or a convenient alternative; it is rather 'a new name'[6] given to the Son that He may reveal it to His followers and keep them

[1] Berakoth, 40b.
[2] John xvii. 6.
[3] John xvii. 11.
[4] John xvii. 12.
[5] John xvii. 26.
[6] Rev. ii. 17.

## The Father's Name

in it, making all one in the one great family of God their Father.

It is interesting also to notice that in this prayer we have the term 'hallow' or 'sanctify,' used, however, not in connection with the Name of the Father but with reference to the Son and His disciples. 'For their sakes I sanctify myself, that they themselves also may be sanctified in truth.'[1] So also our Lord prays, 'Sanctify them in the truth: thy word is truth.'[2] Such sanctification is, no doubt, primarily personal, but it is also altruistic and progressive. We can thus see that the petition, 'May thy name be sanctified,' as taught by our Lord, is meant to be something more than a prayer merely for personal holiness in the heart of the individual. The more we desire and pray for our own growth in holiness, our own 'consecration,' the more we realise the far-reaching nature of this prayer with its sublime unselfishness. Our holiness before God is not merely our own private concern, it is of value also for its wider, social aspects, as promoting the progress of the Kingdom. Thus in the Sermon on the Mount our Lord enjoins upon His followers, 'Let your light so shine before men, that they may see your good works, and glorify your Father which is in heaven.'[3]

[1] John xvii. 19.  [2] John xvii. 17.
[3] Matt. v. 16.

## The Lord's Prayer

In this connection it is worth remembering that not only is the Name of the Divine Father glorified by men in expressions of worship and thanksgiving, but God Himself is said to ' glorify ' His Name. Thus in the Fourth Gospel our Lord prays to His Father in the words : ' Glorify thy name.'[1] The answer to this prayer was given, we are told, by ' a voice out of heaven, saying, I have both glorified it and will glorify it again.'[2] It is difficult not to see here a reference to the Divine Fatherhood. The glory of God consists in giving to men the filial spirit, the Spirit of the Son, whereby they feel God to be their Father. The Fourth Gospel is most emphatic in maintaining that the glory of the Father and of the Son is one and mutual, for the Father glorifies the Son by His loving care, and the Son glorifies the Father by His loving obedience. The most glorious act of Sonship is the death upon the Cross whereby He was made ' perfect through sufferings.'[3] In the account of the Betrayal of our Lord, as given in the Fourth Gospel, we are told that, after the departure of Judas from the upper room, ' Jesus saith, Now is the Son of man glorified, and God is glorified in him.'[4] It is in times of great distress and mental conflict, when His ' soul ' is ' troubled,' that the Son of God glorifies

[1] John xii. 28.  [2] *Ibid.*
[3] Heb. ii. 10.  [4] John xii. 31.

## The Father's Name

the name of the Divine Father by His obedience. Thus we find that in this Gospel our Lord prays in the words, 'Father, the hour is come; glorify thy Son, that the Son may glorify thee';[1] and again, 'I glorified thee on the earth, having accomplished the work which thou hast given me to do.'[2] Further, when making supplication for His disciples, He prays, 'Keep them in thy name which thou hast given me, that they may be one, even as we are.'[3] 'The glory which thou hast given me I have given unto them.'[4] The prayer ends with the words, 'O righteous Father, the world knew thee not, but I knew thee; and these know that thou didst send me; and I made known unto them thy name, and will make it known; that the love wherewith thou lovedst me may be in them, and I in them.'[5]

These quotations have here been given in full in order to show how this long, intercessory prayer of our Lord which is recorded in the Fourth Gospel expounds and illuminates the brief petition which He bade His disciples pray, 'Hallowed be thy name.' The example of the Son of Man is valid for all mankind. His life and death were a complete 'hallowing' of the Divine Name, a most sacred revelation of the Fatherhood of God. To the precept

[1] John xvii. 1.
[2] John xvii. 4.
[3] John xvii. 11.
[4] John xvii. 22.
[5] John xvii. 25 f.

## The Lord's Prayer

'Ye shall be holy, for I am holy,'[1] is added the pattern of the sinless Christ whereby we may be perfect, even as the 'heavenly Father is perfect.'[2]

The first petition of the Lord's Prayer is thus universal and all-inclusive, a true missionary prayer that the Name of God may be made known to all men: for wherever the love of the Father is proclaimed and known, the Kingdom is come; and whenever the message of the Divine Fatherhood is received into the hearts of men and realised, 'glorified,' in a life of loving obedience, the Will of God is done. It is therefore evident that it is not in the conventional language of devout aspiration, but in the truest filial piety, that we pray 'Hallowed be thy name,' believing that our Lord Himself in His own prayers to His heavenly Father used the words, 'Glorify thy name.'

The Fourth Gospel also serves to emphasise the character of this petition as a prayer for unity, that the household of God may be one in mind and purpose. 'In that day shall the Lord be one and his name one,' says the prophet Zechariah[3]; and in the same spirit our Lord is represented as praying for His followers, 'Keep them in thy name which thou hast given me, that they may be one, even as we

[1] Lev. xi. 45.  [2] Matt. v. 48.
[3] Zech. xiv. 9.

## The Father's Name

are.'[1] He rejoices that during His lifetime He has kept together the little band of faithful friends to whom He had revealed the Father's Name; 'I manifested thy name unto the men whom thou gavest me out of the world.'[2] 'While I was with them, I kept them in thy name, and I guarded them, and not one of them perished, but the son of perdition.'[3] Only the traitor had forfeited his place in the family of the Divine Father. We may thus regard this petition as being not only a prayer for the expansion of the Gospel and the further declaration of God's Name, but also a prayer for reunion, that the Church may be one, and that as fellow-Christians, in spite of our various denominations, as we term them, we may come to realise, by associated effort to promote God's Kingdom and by sincere prayer for forgiveness, that the one name whereby we may be saved is that of Christ our Lord, who was Himself, by His life and by His death, the 'glory' of the Father's Name.

[1] John xvii. 11.
[2] John xvii. 6.
[3] John xvii. 12.

## CHAPTER V

# The Kingdom of the Father

*'Thy kingdom come.'*—Matt. vi. 10.
*'Fellow-workers unto the kingdom of God.'*
—Col. iv. 11.

*THE* sovereignty of God was a familiar conception in Jewish religious thought at the time of our Lord. The prophets of the Old Testament had frequently spoken of a Kingdom of God which was to come. Zechariah, for example, in his vision of the 'Day of the Lord,' proclaims, 'The Lord shall be king over all the earth.'[1] 'The Lord reigneth' is the message of hope in psalmist and prophet alike. In Apocalyptic writings this idea receives further emphasis—the greater the dissatisfaction with the kingdoms of this world the more eagerly is the Divine government anticipated, when 'the God of heaven shall set up a kingdom which shall never be destroyed.'[2] Our Lord, then, asked no new thing of His followers when He bade them pray for the coming of the Kingdom of God. We may say, in fact, that in this one short petition 'the hopes and fears of all the years' are met. Wherever men have looked for the advent of a King

[1] Zech. xiv. 9.  [2] Dan. ii. 44.

# The Kingdom of the Father

who 'shall reign in righteousness,'[1] or an ideal republic where true justice and real happiness may be found, they have breathed the prayer 'Thy kingdom come.'

Are we, then, to regard the precept of Christ, 'When ye pray, say, Thy kingdom come,' as merely an endorsement of man's natural optimism? There is surely a more definite, a more forcible meaning in the prayer. The Jew had always a vivid picture before his mind's eye when he prayed for the coming Kingdom or reign of God. The sufferings of the Jewish nation under foreign rule during the centuries which preceded the birth of our Lord invigorated and intensified the keen expectation of a coming 'theocracy.' Thus, to quote once again from the Book of Daniel, it is said, 'The kingdom and the dominion, and the greatness of the kingdoms under the whole heaven, shall be given to the people of the saints of the Most High: his kingdom is an everlasting kingdom, and all dominions shall serve and obey him. Here is the end of the matter.'[2] And moreover, for the furtherance of this Kingdom, the nation of Israel was to do her share: 'The people that know their God shall be strong and do exploits.'[3] Those, therefore, who heard our Lord when, after the imprisonment of the Baptist, He

---

[1] Isa. xxxii. 1.    [2] Dan. vii. 27.
[3] Dan. xi. 32.

# The Lord's Prayer

proclaimed 'The time is fulfilled, and the kingdom of God is at hand,'[1] would give a very definite content to His message.

That their interpretation was partial, in that it was largely secular, political, and national, is obvious to all who read the Gospel story. The Temptation of our Lord shows plainly how He Himself discarded such incomplete and erroneous conceptions of the Kingdom of His Father. Throughout His ministry our Lord was ever challenging and correcting the prevailing opinions as to the nature and methods of the Kingdom, explaining its true character by His teaching and by His life. Both the Sermon on the Mount and the Death upon the Cross are a revaluation, a restatement of the philosophy of the Kingdom, a revelation of its 'mystery.' We cannot indeed forget that the form which Christ gave to His teaching was 'the gospel of the kingdom,'[2] the good news of God's reign. By so doing He touched a responsive chord in the soul of the nation. It was by means of their hopes and deep desires that He appealed to them and wished to help them, drawing them 'with the bands of love.'[3] When He spoke to His audience of the 'Kingdom of heaven,' He was sure of their attention, for His subject was of supreme interest to all who heard Him. If they would receive it, it was a 'gospel,' a joyous

[1] Mark i. 15.  [2] Matt. iv. 23, etc.  [3] Hos. xi. 4.

## The Kingdom of the Father

message for them all, the glad tidings of the Divine Fatherhood, that the 'theocracy,' the Rule of God, is realised and finds its full expression in the love of God for man and of man for his neighbour. The Kingdom is indeed the Sovereignty of Love. It therefore follows that we best interpret the first three clauses of the Lord's Prayer, if we bear in mind that they are inseparably connected and cannot be considered in isolation from one another. The sacred ideal which the Prayer sets before us is the hallowing of the Divine Name, Father, which is achieved by means of a kingdom, the rule of the heavenly Father, whose will is thus performed ' on earth, as it is in heaven.' The Lord's Prayer is often spoken of as the ' Prayer of the Kingdom.' It is, perhaps, more properly described as the ' Prayer of the Divine Fatherhood,' the ' Paternoster,' the ' Our Father.'

We may here remark that the message of the Kingdom, the Gospel of Hope, takes its start from ' the earth, our habitation.'[1] It is no mere realm of ideas, of things-in-themselves, or of supra-terrestrial blessedness. Nor is it a Utopia, an Erewhon, or Nowhere, for it is not only potential but actual, here and now. In the later writers of Apocalypse we can see that there is a tendency to despair of any regeneration of this earth and of this our present humanity,

[1] Bp. Butler, *Analogy of Religion*, c. iii.

# The Lord's Prayer

so that the vision of the older prophets is forgotten, in which the earth would be 'full of the knowledge of the Lord, as the waters cover the sea.'[1] Our Lord, however, as the Son of Man, is primarily concerned with the needs of humanity. No doubt the sign of the Son of Man will be displayed resplendent in the heavens, but His work is to be seen here upon earth among His fellow-men, for He says of Himself that He 'came to seek and to save that which was lost.'[2] So too He declares, 'If I by the finger of God cast out devils, then is the kingdom of God come upon you.'[3] Even such sacred institutions as the Sabbath must be judged by their real value for mankind, for 'the Son of Man is Lord of the sabbath.'[4] The true 'evidences' for the Kingdom of Heaven are the works of mercy which are done on earth—'the blind receive their sight, and the lame walk, the lepers are cleansed, and the deaf hear, and the dead are raised up, and the poor have good tidings preached to them.' Thus heaven is demonstrated upon earth, and, as we ask for the coming of the Kingdom, we pray 'Thy will be done, as in heaven, so on earth.'

The Gospel of Hope, then, is also the Gospel of Endeavour, of resolution and effort. The

[1] Isa. xi. 9, Hab. ii. 14.
[2] Luke xix. 10.
[3] Luke xi. 20.
[4] Luke vi. 5.
[5] Matt. xi. 5.

## The Kingdom of the Father

disciple is not to sit still, watching and waiting for the Kingdom of his Master, but to put his shoulder to the wheel, or, in other words, to 'take up his cross.' When our Lord cleansed the temple, we are told in the Fourth Gospel that 'His disciples remembered that it was written, The zeal of thine house shall eat me up.'[1] Again, our Lord Himself says of His mission, 'I came to cast fire upon the earth; and what will I, if it is already kindled? But I have a baptism to be baptized with; and how am I straitened till it be accomplished!'[2] This fervour of the Christ communicated itself to His followers so that they were able to 'speak boldly' the message of the Gospel. Thus in the Acts we read, 'Now when they beheld the boldness of Peter and John, and had perceived that they were unlearned and ignorant men, they marvelled; and they took knowledge of them, that they had been with Jesus.'[3]

Further, the glad tidings of the Kingdom is no mere gratifying and interesting announcement to be taken or left at will: it is an invitation, 'Come, for all things are now ready.'[4] There is work to be done and every opportunity for service. 'The harvest truly is plenteous, but the labourers are few.'[5] It is no use praying for further labourers unless we are doing our

---

[1] John ii. 17.   [2] Luke xii. 49.   [3] Acts iv. 13.
[4] Matt. xxii. 4.   [5] Matt. ix. 37.

# The Lord's Prayer

share of work. The Gospel of the Divine Humanity is a call to humanity to rouse itself for its salvation. These are 'the days of the Son of Man,'[1] and every man's work is needed. St. Paul, when he speaks of 'the manner of life' which is 'worthy of the gospel of Christ,' exhorts his readers to 'stand fast in one spirit, with one soul striving [lit. "being fellow-athletes"] for the faith of the gospel.'[2] The Kingdom evokes all our energies and sets a new value upon them. Thus, in the language of the Fourth Gospel, 'the light' is given to men that they may 'work.'[3]

'The kingdom of heaven suffereth violence, and men of violence take it by force.'[4] Modern commentators have singularly failed to grasp the true significance of these words. Yet the early monks, the 'Christian athletes,' as they called themselves, rightly apprehended the meaning of this saying.[5] Special occasions call for special measures, and the furtherance of the Kingdom involves unexampled energy and earnestness. The revelation of the 'new name'[6] necessitates new activities and new vision. The Kingdom must 'suffer violence,' be captured,

---

[1] Luke xvii. 22.    [2] Phil. i. 27.
[3] John ix. 4, xi. 9.    [4] Matt. xi. 12.
[5] *Cf.* also Dante:
    'Regnum coelorum violenzia pate
  Da caldo amor e da viva speranza'
               (*Paradiso* xx. 94 f.);
and Bunyan, *Holy War*, c. xvi.    [6] Rev. ii. 17, etc.

# The Kingdom of the Father

like a citadel, by assault. Not without cost and great effort is the 'pearl of great price'[1] to be secured. Nor are these the counsels of perfection with a special blessing reserved for the ascetic warrior above and beyond his fellow-men. St. Luke preserves a variant of this saying which is not a mere mistaken paraphrase, as some have thought. 'The gospel of the kingdom of God is preached, and every man entereth violently into it.'[2] The exploit of entering the Kingdom involves for all a degree of violence, of strenuous and enthusiastic activity, the 'hunger and thirst after righteousness.'[3] However much we may emphasise the fact that the Kingdom is the gift of God and comes *from* Him, yet we must show ourselves to be eager for it, it must come *by* us. The utmost courage will thus be needed, and all fear and the misgivings of timidity must be put aside as unworthy. 'No man, having put his hand to the plough, and looking back, is fit for the kingdom of God.'[4] Faith and love will make all things possible. 'Fear not, little flock; for it is your Father's good pleasure to give you the kingdom.'[5] Yet our prayer for the coming of the heavenly Kingdom is imperative, impetrative, and importunate. 'Ask, and it

[1] Matt. xiii. 46.
[2] Luke xvi. 16.
[3] Matt. v. 6.
[4] Luke ix. 62.
[5] Luke xii. 32.

## The Lord's Prayer

shall be given you; seek, and ye shall find; knock, and it shall be opened unto you,'[1] are the degrees of our boldness. Hence we may say that our Lord, when He speaks of the 'violence' of those who force their entry, who are pressing into the Kingdom, is not, as is often alleged, reproaching those who thought of the Messianic blessings as political, and tried to reach them by rebellion and war, or even repressing the unhealthy excitement manifested by certain of His followers, but rather setting His approval upon those who, beginning with St. John the Baptist, would seize at all hazards upon the Kingdom and its treasures.

It is probably in this connection and on these lines that we may best arrive at some solution of the vexed problems of the Gospel eschatology, the picture of the Kingdom which is to come 'with power.'[2] The teaching about the 'Last Things' is not easily understood unless we bear in mind the eagerness and enthusiasm which must characterise all real moral effort, whether individual or social. There is an element of urgency, of immediacy, in all ethic. 'But this I say, brethren, the time is shortened,'[3] is not simply the utterance of a disciple who erroneously believed in an early return of the Master upon the clouds of heaven, it is the cry

[1] Matt. vii. 7, Luke xi. 9.  [2] Mark ix. 1.
[3] 1 Cor. vii. 29.

## The Kingdom of the Father

of all who would do something for the Kingdom of God. The field is so vast and human energies so small, human life so short, that all must feel the need for prompt and definite action, 'the night cometh, when no man can work.'[1]

The Gospel ethic, then, the morality of the Kingdom, is not obscured or overlaid by its eschatology, its pictures of 'the consummation of the age.'[2] The imperative obligation of the laws of conduct is intensified by the visions of the completed Kingdom with its perfect righteousness. The present need of reform is therefore urgent. 'Repent ye, for the Kingdom of heaven is at hand.'[3] Viewed in this light the Beatitudes are not a list of domestic virtues, or a code of genteel behaviour, accepted by those who would abolish dogma, but rather the marching orders for the soldiers of the Kingdom. When men speak of 'the moral equivalent of warfare' they utter a true parable of the Kingdom of God. St. Paul had 'the mind of Christ' when he exhorted his 'son Timothy' to 'fight the good fight of the faith, lay hold on the life eternal, whereunto thou wast called.'[4] As we read the words of our Lord, 'Blessed are the meek: for they shall inherit the earth,'[5] we do well to remember that Moses, the founder of Israel as

---

[1] John ix. 4.  
[2] Matt. xxiv. 3 (R.V. marg.).  
[3] Matt. iv. 17.  
[4] 1 Tim. vi. 12.  
[5] Matt. v. 11.

# The Lord's Prayer

a nation, and a valiant workman for the Kingdom, is represented in the Bible as a 'very meek'[1] man.

We are not to conclude from this that the Gospel of the Kingdom is only a new method of efficiency, a glorification of physical vitality, a doctrine of the Superman, or even an outburst of emotional revivalism, of 'salvationism,' as it is sometimes termed. It is rather the impetus of a magnificent and heroic enthusiasm, imparting a real dynamic force to the precepts of the moral law. Moreover, such a sanction is, as we have seen, always binding, always imperative. The times are ever out of joint, and no one can justly refuse the vocation to set them right. There is no need to talk of an *interimsethik* in the Gospel, a morality of the moment, seeing that the great invitation 'Follow me'[2] is for all time.

At the present day there are those who clamour for 'applied Christianity,' who cry, 'Why not give Christianity a trial?'[3] and we may recognise that Saul has joined the ranks of the prophets, even though much of his message may proclaim him but a 'mad fellow.'[4] The prayer 'Thy kingdom come' is a sincere and whole-hearted yearning to apply the principles of the Gospel of the

[1] Num. xii. 3.  [2] Mark ii. 14, etc.
[3] G. Bernard Shaw, Pref. to *Androcles and the Lion*.
[4] 2 Kings ix. 11.

# The Kingdom of the Father

Divine Fatherhood. The man who is so far interested in Christianity as to 'wish it true' may join in uttering the petition 'Hallowed be thy name,' while he who is honestly anxious to see it 'come true' will pray and work for the realisation of the Kingdom, the rule of God in the hearts of men.

We have here, then, in the religion of the Kingdom a morality touched with a true emotion, the passion for humanity. Individual virtue finds its social value, and devotion can no longer be self-centred. 'Inasmuch as ye did it unto one of these my brethren, even these least, ye did it unto me.'[1] Yet there is nothing of feverish fanaticism in the Gospel urgency. It has a philosophy, a 'mystery of the kingdom,'[2] which does not 'come too late' because it is initial and fundamental. The Divine Wisdom cries, 'Learn of me.'[3] The first thing needed is re-education, a revision of values and standards. We must 'become as little children,'[4] in order that we may challenge and call in question those things which the 'wise and prudent,'[5] the time-worn and sophisticated, take for granted. We shall thus see good and evil, love and fear, riches and poverty, life and death in their true pro-

[1] Matt. xxv. 40.
[2] Mark iv. 11.
[3] Matt. xi. 29.
[4] Matt. xviii. 3.
[5] Matt. xi. 25.

# The Lord's Prayer

portion because our revaluation is in accordance with the great command, 'Seek ye first the kingdom of God.'[1] Hence our resolution, our zeal, is 'according to knowledge'[2] as being the outcome of due deliberation. 'For which of you, desiring to build a tower, doth not first sit down and count the cost?'[3] The moral warfare demands a careful consideration of the forces at our disposal. 'What king, as he goeth to encounter another king in war, will not sit down first and take counsel whether he is able with ten thousand to meet him that cometh against him with twenty thousand?'[4] Calculation is concerned, not with rewards or 'thrones' in heaven, but with our ability 'to be baptized with the baptism' of the Master Himself.[5]

Once again, the fact that 'the kingdom of God is within you'[6] does not mean that it is to remain there. Growth, expansion, penetration are essential characteristics of the Kingdom, as illustrated by the parables of the Mustard Seed, the Leaven, and the earth which brings forth 'first the blade, then the ear, then the full corn in the ear.'[7] All devotion, therefore, must find its natural outlet, and even

---

[1] Matt. vi. 33.
[2] Rom. x. 2.
[3] Luke xiv. 28.
[4] Luke xiv. 31.
[5] Mark x. 38.
[6] Luke xvii. 21.
[7] Mark iv. 28.

# The Kingdom of the Father

the man with only one talent must put it out at interest. For indeed the spacious realm of God is not to be cramped either by an individualistic quietism or an excessive 'other-worldliness,' much less by an obsession of imminent catastrophe. The Kingdom of God is for all men, if they will enter it, and it is for all time. Thus it is rooted in the past, in the vision of the prophet, the moral hopefulness of the law-giver, and the faith of the psalmist, while it takes its energy, its overwhelming impetus from the crying needs of the present. It has also a wide future with boundless possibilities, for it is a process actively working towards its consummation. Meanwhile our task is service, following in the footsteps of our Master. 'Whosoever would become great among you, shall be your minister: and whosoever would be first among you, shall be servant of all. For verily the Son of Man came not to be ministered unto, but to minister, and to give his life a ransom for many.'[1] We would not be amongst those who cry 'The Lord delayeth his coming,'[2] and so relax our moral resolution and our social efforts, but rather be found among those 'men of violence' by means of whom God is pleased to hasten the Kingdom.

It is however, quite natural that those who

[1] Mark x. 45.      [2] Matt. xxiv. 48.

## The Lord's Prayer

pray for the coming of God's Kingdom should sometimes ask ' How long ? '[1] ' When shall these things be ? '[2] The only answer to the question is to be found in the words of our Lord, ' Of that day or that hour knoweth no one, not even the angels in heaven, neither the Son, but the Father. Take ye heed, watch and pray : for ye know not when the time is.'[3] Are we then to say that the apocalyptic picture of the End has no value, as being entirely imaginary ? There can be no doubt that our Lord as prophet used the language and the symbols of prophecy, yet such language must have a meaning. Further, as a prophet, He was concerned with the events of human history, and we find in those events at any rate a partial fulfilment. Much of His prophetic vision was fulfilled in the Fall of Jerusalem which He had predicted. In all great national or world crises ' these things must needs come to pass.'[4] ' But the end is not yet,'[5] even when we allow for such manifestations of the Coming. There is still conflict, and the ' one Divine event ' is still interpreted as ' far off.' Nor does it suffice to say that the Kingdom has come, inasmuch as it is ' within ' us, or to maintain that in the lifetime of each generation, not to say each individual, ' all these things are

[1] Rev. vi. 10.
[2] Matt. xxiv. 3.
[3] Mark xiii. 32.
[4] Matt. xxiv. 6.
[5] *Ibid.*

## The Kingdom of the Father

fulfilled.'[1] We have only to look around us to see that there is as yet no Kingdom among us, achieved ' on earth, as in heaven.' With regard, however, to the time of the End, it is as true as ever to say that ' no one knoweth.'[2] Science gives us no help, she in her turn can only prophesy. Yet we feel that an end must come. Underlying the Christian belief in the Second Advent is the sure conviction that it is not ethical to assume that good and evil will continue for ever balancing each other. A permanent dualism cannot be completely ethical. A God of Righteousness means that some day righteousness will prevail as a world-order. And the victory must surely be where the battle is. Earth is the battle-ground of conflict and it is doubtless fitting that earth also should be the field of the ultimate victory. Yet neither place nor time can be primary considerations when we remember that the Kingdom of Heaven is ' life eternal.'[3]

We need not indeed perplex ourselves with questions of ' times and seasons,'[4] and ' lo, here! or, there!'[5] Our duty is plain, and the uncertainty of the future only makes it the more obvious. 'Take ye heed, watch and pray: for ye know not when the time is, lest coming suddenly he find you sleeping.'[6] It is, perhaps,

[1] Matt. xxiv. 34.  [2] Mark xiii. 32.  [3] John iv. 36, etc.
[4] Acts i. 7.  [5] Luke xvii. 21.  [6] Mark xiii. 33, 36.

## The Lord's Prayer

the suddenness of the Second Coming which is the most prominent feature in the Gospel picture of the End. This is further emphasised by the language of the Book of Revelation, ' If therefore thou shalt not watch, I will come as a thief, and thou shalt not know what hour I will come upon thee.'[1] And, as a matter of fact, whatever may be the manner of the End, we can see that here and now progress in the Kingdom often comes suddenly, unexpectedly, an advance *per saltum*. History never repeats itself exactly; the unexpected emerges, for ' the Kingdom of God cometh not with observation,'[2] by nicely calculated degrees. And if history is not an exact science, neither is psychology. Conversion, for example, is never calculable, and the moral life is full of surprises : there is no such thing in ethics as a fixed character. Hence the Kingdom can never lose its romance, its faith.

Further, to be instant in prayer for the coming of the Kingdom, to 'watch and pray,'[3] requires the strong perseverance of faith. ' He that endureth to the end, the same shall be saved.'[4] The great consideration is that each man shall be found at his post, working at his appointed task for the furtherance of the Kingdom. ' Blessed is that servant, whom his Lord when

---

[1] Rev. iii. 3.  
[2] Luke xvii. 20.  
[3] Mark. xiii. 33, etc.  
[4] Matt. x. 22.

## The Kingdom of the Father

he cometh shall find so doing.'[1] Watchfulness, perseverance, and unfailing faith are thus required of all who would ' enter into the joy '[2] of their Master. ' Howbeit, when the Son of Man cometh, shall he find faith on the earth ? '[3] It is possible that our want of faith delays the coming of the Kingdom, while it is certain that we can take no step forward without it. For the Christian to surrender faith, to desert his post, is to betray the Kingdom, to be false to God and man.

It is often said that the Fourth Gospel takes but slight account of the Gospel of the Kingdom, that little or no eschatology, for example, is to be found in its pages, and that the very phrases ' Kingdom of God ' and ' Son of Man ' seem to be consciously avoided. It is also asserted that the enthusiasm of earlier days has vanished, has been displaced by the placidity of local Church life: the only ' violence ' which remains is that of dialectic, of heated controversy with Jewish opponents. The grand passion for humanity, it is alleged, has dwindled and contracted into the gentler and less exacting love of ' the brethren.'[4] Yet we should be cautious in our exposition of this Gospel, remembering that it is itself, in some degree, an ' interpretation ' of the Christ and His life and death in the light of early

[1] Matt. xxiv. 46.   [2] Matt. xxv. 21.   [3] Luke xviii. 8.
[4] 1 John iii. 14–16; *cf.* John xxi. 23.

# The Lord's Prayer

Christian experience. Our Lord's teaching was many-sided and His disciples were men of varied mentality. Hence in their presentation of the Gospel, there is always a question of emphasis, one note may sound clearer than another.. Thus in the Fourth Gospel the bright colours of the apocalyptic picture have certainly faded, but the central figure of the Saviour stands out the more clearly. Enthusiasm for the Kingdom has become devotion to the King. 'Lord, to whom shall we go? thou hast the words of eternal life.'[1] Yet this is not a false or even, necessarily, a one-sided development. Our Lord indeed in the Synoptic Gospels declares, 'Whosoever shall lose his life *for my sake* and the gospel's shall save it.'[2] Similarly, He promises to those who renounce kinsfolk or possessions '*for my sake*, and for the gospel's sake,' that they will be recompensed 'a hundredfold now in this time,' and will receive 'in the world to come eternal life.'[3] It is to be noticed that the use of the expression 'life,' or 'eternal life,' which in the Fourth Gospel seems to take the place of the phrase 'the kingdom of God,' is not peculiar to that Gospel, but occurs throughout the New Testament, though not, it must be admitted, with the same frequency. There is a passage, for example, in St. Mark where 'to enter into life' and 'to enter into the kingdom of God' are

[1] John vi. 68.  [2] Mark viii. 35.  [3] Mark x. 29.

# The Kingdom of the Father

used as synonymous terms.[1] Both, it is shown, involve renunciation, a 'cutting off,' or 'casting away.' Again, it is in the spirit of the Synoptists, if not in their exact language, that the Fourth Gospel records the saying, 'He that loveth his life loseth it; and he that hateth his life in this world shall keep it unto life eternal. If any man serve me, let him follow me.'[2] Thus 'to have eternal life' no less than 'to enter the kingdom' demands devotion and renunciation, and on this all four Gospels are agreed. Further, the command 'to love one another' involves sacrifice, —may even require the surrender of life itself; 'This is my commandment, that ye love one another, even as I have loved you. Greater love hath no man than this, that a man lay down his life for his friends.'[3] Such loving service, inspired by a fervent devotion to the Master, is, it must surely be conceded, no unworthy interpretation of the Kingdom. Wherever such love is manifested, we cannot say that there is a decline of enthusiasm.

We have also to bear in mind that the 'Dualism,' as it is called, of this Gospel implies militancy, 'not peace, but a sword,'—to use the language of the earlier Evangelists.[4] God and the devil, light and darkness, spirit and flesh, life and death, are antithetical and combative.

---

[1] Mark ix. 43–47.  [2] John xii. 25.  [3] John xv. 12 f.
[4] Matt. x. 34; *cf.* Luke xii. 51.

# The Lord's Prayer

Thus for man the world is a battlefield, a conflict for the victory of life and love. 'In the world ye shall have tribulation : but be of good cheer, I have overcome the world.'[1] The First Epistle is a commentary on the Gospel when it declares, 'For whatsoever is begotten of God overcometh the world : and this is the victory that hath overcome the world, even our faith.'[2]

The peaceful coming of the Spirit, we are told by many Gospel critics, is the Johannine counterpart to the apocalyptic Parousia of the Synoptists. The gentle comfort and exhortation of the Paraclete take the place of the alarms and panic of the Second Advent. It must not be forgotten, however, that the outpouring of the Spirit is an idea which is eschatological in origin and that it never entirely loses that significance. The Prophet Joel had foretold, in his vision of 'the day of the Lord,' that 'it shall come to pass afterward, that I will pour out my spirit upon all flesh ; and your sons and your daughters shall prophesy, your old men shall dream dreams, your young men shall see visions : and also upon the servants and upon the handmaids in those days I will pour out my spirit. And I will shew wonders in the heavens and in the earth, blood, and fire, and pillars of smoke.'[3] On the day of Pentecost St. Peter in his oration quotes from this passage, and the words of the prophet must

[1] John xvi. 33.  [2] 1 John v. 4.  [3] Joel ii. 28–30.

The Kingdom of the Father
always have recurred to the minds of the first Christians when an outpouring of the Spirit was promised to them. Thus the Spirit was expected to come 'with power.'[1] The Fourth Gospel, while, no doubt, it corrects extravagant hopes and fancies by its sober presentation of the 'Spirit of truth,'[2] yet plainly demonstrates the active dynamic energies of the Holy Ghost. 'The wind bloweth where it listeth, and thou hearest the voice thereof, but knowest not whence it cometh, and whither it goeth: so is every one that is born of the Spirit.'[3] The promise of the Spirit illuminates the whole prospect of the future. 'Let not your heart be troubled, neither let it be afraid.'[4] There is no cause for shrinking or timidity, for the Paraclete is to come. The 'glorification' of the Son of Man and His ascension are the prelude to a new epoch, the dispensation of the Spirit. His task will be to impart fuller knowledge, to revive memory, and to stimulate new activities. The disciple may even rival the Master,—'Greater works than these shall he do; because I go to the Father.'[5] The Holy Spirit is to be regarded as 'another Comforter' who will encourage to fresh conquests in the victory over the world. He will 'guide' the disciples 'into all truth,'[6]

[1] *Cf*. Acts i. 8, x. 38.  [2] John xv. 26.
[3] John iii. 8.  [4] John xiv. 27.
[5] John xiv. 12.  [6] John xvi. 13.

## The Lord's Prayer

including moral truth, or, as we might say, will lead them to 'the kingdom of heaven and its righteousness.'[1] The future is thus, by the power of the Spirit, an era of progress and development towards the fuller attainment of 'life eternal,' the knowledge of the Fatherhood of God. 'And this is life eternal, that they might know thee the only true God, and him whom thou didst send, even Jesus Christ.'[2] Nor is the message for the faithful only, it is for the whole world. 'I, if I be lifted up from the earth, will draw all men unto myself.'[3] There is here again no diminution of the early enthusiasm, no loss of the 'first love,'[4] but a true revelation of 'the mysteries of the kingdom,'[5] the loving sovereignty of God.

We have now to ask whether our Lord Himself in His own prayers, prayed for the coming of the Kingdom? We might naturally expect that, as the Founder of that Kingdom, He would pray, as indeed He worked and died, for its promotion. Yet in the prayers of our Lord which are recorded for us in the Gospels we do not find that He prays the actual words 'Thy kingdom come.' It is, of course, possible that He did not choose to join His followers in praying 'Give us the Kingdom,' just as

---

[1] Matt. vi. 33.  
[2] John xvii. 3.  
[3] John xii. 32.  
[4] Rev. ii. 4.  
[5] Matt. xiii. 11.

## The Kingdom of the Father

He will not say 'Our Father,' but 'My Father,' or 'your Father.' Thus we find that He sometimes speaks of 'My Kingdom,' as in St. Luke, where we read 'Ye are they which have continued with me in my temptations; and I appoint unto you a kingdom, even as my Father appointed unto me, that ye may eat and drink at my table in my kingdom.'[1] Again, in the Fourth Gospel, our Lord replies to the question of Pilate, 'Art thou the King of the Jews?' 'My kingdom is not of this world: if my kingdom were of this world, then would my servants fight, that I should not be delivered to the Jews: but now is my kingdom not from hence.'[2] So also He turns to His disciples and says 'Fear not, little flock; for it is *your* Father's good pleasure to give *you* the kingdom.'[3] Hence, it may be, He will not pray in company with His disciples 'Thy kingdom come.'

A reason for this is, perhaps, also to be found in the fact that He occupies a unique position in the Kingdom. He is the Founder of the Kingdom, not merely an aspirant for admission. It is not so much that He thinks of Himself as Supreme King, for the Kingdom is 'of God,'—it is 'the kingdom of the Father,'[4]— as that He feels the Kingdom to be within Him. Thus when He declares, 'The kingdom

---

[1] Luke xxii. 28 f.  [2] John xviii. 33, 36.
[3] Luke xii. 32.    [4] Matt. xiii. 43.

# The Lord's Prayer

of heaven is within you,'[1] He is speaking from His own consciousness. He is aware that the Kingdom is already established in His own heart, and is being realised in the hearts of His followers.

Yet such suppositions are, at best, conjectural. Even in His own heart the Kingdom was liable to assault. Temptation was always possible, and even after the victory in the wilderness, alternatives could still present themselves, the choice between 'all the kingdoms of the world, and the glory of them,'[2] and obedience to His Father's will. Thus, though we are not told that our Lord prayed the prayer 'Thy kingdom come,' yet we find that He uses the petition 'Thy will be done,' the necessary accompaniment of such a prayer. The Father's will must determine the principles and methods of the Kingdom which His Son was sent to proclaim. 'Not my will, but thine, be done.'[3] Even the Messiah, the Founder of the Kingdom, God's Vicegerent, must pray in time of trial and temptation lest, by saving His life, He forfeit His soul and with it the Kingdom. The fate of the Kingdom was determined in the agony of Gethsemane, and it was prayer that decided the battle. 'Thou didst open the kingdom of heaven to all believers' is our triumph-song of thankfulness.

[1] Luke xvii. 21.   [2] Matt. iv. 8.   [3] Luke xxii. 42.

## The Kingdom of the Father

If our Lord could pray for the fulfilment of the Divine Will at whatever cost, He could also heartily rejoice when He witnessed the accomplishment of that will in the successful promotion of the Kingdom. Thus in the Prayer of Thanksgiving, recorded by St. Matthew and St. Luke, our Lord gives thanks for the proclamation of the Gospel of the Kingdom by His disciples and for the fact that His Father has revealed its mysteries to 'babes.'[1] In this He sees a striking evidence of the fulfilment of the Divine will. 'Even so, Father, for so it seemed good in thy sight,'—in other words, it was 'the Father's good pleasure to give the kingdom'[2] to those who had 'become as little children.'[3] We can here hardly avoid the conclusion that our Lord had prayed earnestly for this 'coming' of the Kingdom. The Prayer of Thanksgiving seems to be one of deep gratitude for answered prayers, for the success which has crowned not only the efforts of the disciples, but also the prayers and counsels of the Master. In the power of the Holy Spirit our Lord utters His joyful prayer of thankfulness for the justification of His hopes and plans, His selection and training of the disciples,—in a word, the response to His prayers for the Kingdom.

[1] Matt. xi. 25 f, Luke x. 21.  [2] Luke xii. 32.
[3] Matt. xviii. 3.

## The Lord's Prayer

The long intercessory prayer which is given in the Fourth Gospel has, it must be observed, no direct mention of the Kingdom. Yet the authority of the Son to confer 'eternal life,' that is to say, the right of admission to the Kingdom, is affirmed. 'Thou hast given him authority over all flesh, that whatsoever thou hast given him, to them he should give eternal life.'[1] We are reminded of the similar declaration of authority which follows the Prayer of Thanksgiving. 'All things have been delivered unto me of my Father: and no one knoweth the Son, save the Father; neither doth any know the Father save the Son, and he to whomsoever the Son willeth to reveal him.'[2] Further, the work of the Son upon earth has been fulfilled, 'I have glorified thee on the earth: I have finished the work which thou gavest me to do.'[3] Thus the Divine Name has been glorified, the Divine Will performed, the Divine Kingdom founded. The prayer is also concerned with the future of the Kingdom after the death of the Founder. We have already pointed out that the Lord's Prayer may be regarded as the great Family Prayer, and here we find that our Lord Himself prays for His followers as the family of the heavenly Father. 'Holy Father, keep them in thy name which

---

[1] John xvii. 2.     [2] Matt. xi. 27, Luke x. 22
[3] John xvii. 4.

# The Kingdom of the Father

thou hast given me, that they may be one, even as we are.'[1] So again, 'The glory which thou hast given me I have given unto them; that they may be perfected into one; that the world may know that thou didst send me, and lovedst them, even as thou lovedst me. Father, that which thou hast given me, I will that, where I am, they also may be with me.'[2] The family is of wide extent. 'Neither for these only do I make request, but for them also that believe on me through their word; that they may all be one; even as thou, Father, art in me, and I in thee, that they also may be in us.'[3] The aim and end of the Kingdom is thus declared to be union. The Kingdom is of God and unto God, begins and ends with God, 'that,' in St. Paul's words, 'God may be all in all.'[4] We have therefore in this prayer of intercession, which the Fourth Gospel sets before us, a real prayer for the Kingdom, a true memory, no doubt, of the mind of Christ as He prayed for the Kingdom which He loved and for which He died.

[1] John xvii. 11.
[2] John xvii. 22-24.
[3] John xvii. 20-21.
[4] 1 Cor. xv. 28.

CHAPTER VI

## The Will of the Father

*'Thy will be done, as in heaven, so on earth.'*
—Matt. vi. 10.
*'We are God's fellow-workers.'*—1 Cor. iii. 9.

*T*HE expositions and interpretations of this clause in the Lord's Prayer have been almost bewildering in their variety. Thus it has been explained by some as an aspiration of devout and humble submission, by others as an assertion of the pre-eminently ethical character of the Kingdom, by others as an heroic resolve to do God's service at all costs, to follow the argument of the Divine purpose wherever it may lead. Yet all these, we feel, are only aspects, points of view, partial explanations. The petition, as used by our Lord Himself and taught by Him to His followers, has a wider meaning. The will of God, the purpose of God for man, is, as St. Paul reminds us, a 'mystery,'[1] difficult of apprehension, but capable of revelation, and therefore a matter for prayer.

We would first notice that the words, 'Thy will be done, as in heaven, so on earth,' are

---
[1] Eph. i. 9.

# The Will of the Father

vital to the meaning of the whole Lord's Prayer. They are indeed an expression of the very spirit of prayer. 'If we ask anything according to his will, he heareth us.'[1] Hence we may regard this clause as in some sense the climax of the Lord's Prayer, for it expounds, defines, corrects, and illuminates not only the petitions which precede but also those which follow. When the Father's Name has been sanctified in the salvation of His children, and in the establishment of His kingdom, the will of God is fulfilled, while for the doing of that will 'on earth, as in heaven' our daily sustenance is provided, our sins forgiven, and power granted to overcome temptation. We shall surely therefore be justified in deciding that this petition is an original part of the Lord's Prayer, and is not merely a paraphrase added to explain the preceding clause, the prayer for the Kingdom, in an ethical sense. Yet it may be asked, Why are these words only to be found in St. Matthew's version of the Prayer and not recorded by St. Luke? The reason is, as we shall seek to prove elsewhere, that St. Luke decided to omit this petition for the performance of the Divine Will because of its liability to misinterpretation. If, as we shall discover, there were reasons strong enough in his opinion to warrant his omission of this clause, we are the more

[1] 1 John v. 14.

## The Lord's Prayer

firmly convinced that it formed an original part of the prayer which our Lord taught to His disciples.

In considering the meaning of this clause it may very possibly be suggested that if we would 'breathe the prayer divinely taught, Thy will be done,' we must modify considerably, if not abandon entirely, that view of the Kingdom which we have set forth. There is here, it will be said, little room for that spirit of adventure, that ardent enthusiasm, that 'violence,' which we saw to be a leading characteristic of the Kingdom. Yet we have already intimated that resignation is not the only possible interpretation of this petition, and that the lesson of submission is only one of many 'doctrines' to be learned from the doing of 'the will.'[1] The will of the Father's love is purposive, resolute, requiring the active co-operation of man's will. 'Our wills are ours to make them Thine' is a much-quoted sentiment, yet we must see that they are worth the offering. For indeed the will to believe, to trust, to do, is the essential condition of the great enterprise of the Kingdom.

It will thus be seen that this petition is a corrective of apathy and indifference, of wilful ignorance, of moral dulness, of social indolence. 'Soul, take thine ease'[2] can never be said by those who pray aright 'Thy will be done.' Our

[1] John vii. 17     [2] Luke xii. 19.

## The Will of the Father

Lord teaches us that the Sabbath was made for man, but God has no day of rest. 'My Father worketh hitherto, and I work.'[1] It is our duty therefore to let God work through our wills and our activities. Man indeed must co-operate with God and with his neighbour if he would love either of them truly. There is no higher dignity given to men than to be 'God's fellow-workers,'[2] while there is no more grievous condemnation than the judgment of the Hebrew oracle, 'Curse ye Meroz, said the angel of the Lord, curse ye bitterly the inhabitants thereof; because they came not to the help of the Lord.'[3] It is not so much by claiming that God is on our side that we enter the Kingdom as by seeing that we are on His side. We do not call God down from heaven to march with our armies, for the ark of the Lord may fall into the hands of the enemy, but we go forth with His hosts.

Our watchword, our battle-cry, is given us, 'As in heaven, so on earth,' and we 'march breast forward.'[4] The song of the angels is ours, 'Glory to God in the highest, and on earth peace among men of His good will.'[5] Thus we labour for peace, not in the quiescence of world-weariness, but in the victory of God and His Kingdom. 'Unto us a child is born, unto us a son is given,'

---

[1] John v. 17.  
[2] I Cor. iii. 9.  
[3] Judges v. 23.  
[4] R. Browning, *Epilogue*.  
[5] Luke ii. 14.

# The Lord's Prayer

and 'of the increase of his government and of peace there shall be no end.'[1] The spirit of the prayer 'Thy will be done' is 'the spirit of counsel and might,'[2] for the first intention of this petition is not that it should be a cry to God to enable us to endure and to submit, to be meek and patient, but rather that, as in heaven all sorrow and sighing are fled away, so here on earth we should feel the joy of service. It is a prayer to God that 'we may cheerfully accomplish those things that thou wouldest have done'[3] with the ready service of the angels for our example.

Co-operation is thus the true consummation of obedience. The will of God was never more truly ethical than in the laws of the Gospel. Faith without works is void, and it is not enough to cry 'Lord, Lord,'[4] for the Kingdom of Heaven requires that we shall do the Father's will. 'If ye love me, ye will keep my commandments.'[5] The Jew was to have no monopoly of morality. 'For I say unto you, that except your righteousness shall exceed the righteousness of the scribes and Pharisees, ye shall in no wise enter the kingdom of heaven.'[6] Yet the Gospel message is more than ethics or a revelation of God's will in moral precepts.

---

[1] Isa. ix. 6 f.     [2] Isa. xi. 2.
[3] Book of Common Prayer, *Collect for Trinity* XX.
[4] Matt. vii. 21.    [5] John xiv. 15.    [6] Matt. v. 20.

## The Will of the Father

'A new commandment I give unto you, that ye love one another; even as I have loved you, that ye also love one another. By this shall all men know that ye are my disciples, if ye have love one to another.'[1] The new element in the Christian law is love. The Jewish legalist because he did not love God as Father did not know where to look for his neighbour. When in his prayers he thought of 'other men' such as 'this publican,'[2] he did not realise that 'it is not the will of your Father which is in heaven, that one of these little ones should perish.'[3] Pharisaic religion was stagnant, vitiated by the 'passive fallacy,' because it had not true love as its motive-power. For, as we have seen, the Kingdom of Heaven is the Sovereignty of Love.

Hence it is that we must investigate our motives, must see that the 'eye be single.'[4] The petition, 'Thy will be done,' is a prayer for knowledge and guidance as well as for power. 'Teach me to do thy will, for thou art my God.'[5] If we would co-operate with God, we shall not first blindly assert our wills and then blindly also resign ourselves to His, but rather seek to know His will as He reveals it. Ignorance may be sin, 'the lie in the soul,' as Plato called it,[6] and we desire to be well-instructed and not

[1] John xiii. 34 f.  
[2] Luke xviii. 11.  
[3] Matt. xviii. 14.  
[4] Matt. vi. 22.  
[5] Ps. xl. 8.  
[6] Plato, *Republic*, 382 c.

# The Lord's Prayer

merely well-intentioned. Thus St. Paul reminds his readers that to set the times aright requires intelligence as well as courage. 'Look therefore carefully how ye walk, not as unwise, but as wise; redeeming the time, because the days are evil. Wherefore be ye not foolish, but understand what the will of the Lord is.'[1] The disciple, says our Lord, must be as a 'scribe well-schooled in the Kingdom of heaven.'[2] 'Behold, I send unto you prophets, and wise men, and scribes,' as the missionaries of the Gospel.[3] Not fervent ignorance, but a knowledge of the Lord and His will is the equipment of the true evangelist.

It follows from this that men of understanding, of moral discernment, will refuse to see in events which are plainly evil a direct evidence of the Divine Will. The same fallacy which regards a fatalistic submission as the highest form of obedience will also consider the acts of God as being more especially storm, earthquake, and fire, and will be keen to detect in all suffering and distress a 'visitation of the Lord.' The will of God, as thus regarded, is the direct enemy of all human progress, and such a travesty of the Gospel message can never win mankind. It is obvious that much of the evil and suffering in the world is the result of human wickedness, of wills

[1] Eph. v. 15–17.   [2] *Cf.* Matt. xiii. 52.
[3] Matt. xxiii. 34.

## The Will of the Father

divorced from God. Human thoughtlessness which neglects the Divine Will of command, human insolence which seeks to over-rule the Divine Will of control, are both active agents of evil. Where causes are demonstrable, it is senseless to cry *kismet*: where man's will is evident, we insult God when we say 'It is His will.' Yet we glorify Himself if, as we see the disastrous effects of man's sin and ignorance, we resolve the more courageously to maintain His will, to work with Him for the redemption of His family.

The problem of suffering has been too often discussed in a paragraph or dismissed in a few sentences. Suffering may be a retribution or it may be a remedy, but in very many cases it is neither. The one outstanding fact as to which there is no question is that the existence of suffering is a call to effort. Before we presume to dilate upon the educative value of suffering or its necessary place in the scheme of things, we should be sure that we are doing our part towards its alleviation. There can be no doubt that we need to feel more completely our corporate responsibility in this matter, and to see the Divine Will in the healing of the sick and the casting out of devils. Progress in the easing of the world's pain has been accomplished neither by acceptance, nor by denial, by purposely ignoring its existence, but by devoted effort, by 'men

## The Lord's Prayer

of violence.' Further, the endurance, no less than the alleviation, of suffering calls for active faith rather than passive obedience. The patience of Job was with his friends, his confidence was in his God. 'At all adventures I will take my flesh in my teeth, and put my life in mine hand. Though he slay me, yet will I wait for him,'[1] are the words of 'the great athlete,' as the early Fathers were wont to call him.

It is obvious, however, that suffering appears to hinder our work for the Kingdom. The 'thorn in the flesh'[2] seems insupportable in view of the claims upon us. But here again contraction may serve to intensify. The littleness of our powers may be as much an inspiration as the fact that 'the time is short.'[3] We will do the most with what we have, and not wrap up our one talent in the napkin of self-absorption, or devout compliance. 'My grace is sufficient for thee'[4] is not to be considered as a grant in compensation but rather as a call to such service as we can still perform. Our taskmaster is not 'an austere man,'[5] but our loving Father, and we will gladly accomplish what His grace allows and therefore enjoins. A little child, to take an illustration, cannot do very much to help his elders in their work and often feels his inability,

---

[1] Job xiii. 14 f. (R.V. marg.).    [2] 2 Cor. xii. 7.
[3] 1 Cor. vii. 29.    [4] 2 Cor. xii. 9.
[5] Luke xix. 21.

## The Will of the Father

yet he is on that account all the more pleased and eager when he finds that in some small things he can be of use, and that his efforts are lovingly accepted. So it is, we may be sure, in the Kingdom of God. Our Lord tells us that even if we have 'few things' we are to be 'faithful' in them.[1] Moreover, the 'violence' which He commends is not to be considered merely in the light of its success, but also in proportion to the difficulties which it overcomes.

The petition 'Thy will be done' is thus a prayer for power, for ability to do our task, while at the same time it is a request for knowledge and Divine guidance. As such, it is essential, as we have seen, to the entire meaning of the Lord's Prayer. The response to our prayers is often the gift of 'the spirit of understanding' rather than any immediate and more particular answer, for 'we know not how to pray as we ought.'[2] Yet for this very reason we will be the more instant in prayer, inasmuch as we would grow in knowledge. Thus the Collect in our Prayer Book combines these two aspects of the petition in the words 'Grant that we may both perceive and know what things we ought to do, and also may have grace and power faithfully to fulfil the same.'[3] We pray for a knowledge of God's Will that we may know what

[1] Matt. xxv. 21.     [2] Rom. viii. 26.
[3] Book of Common Prayer, *Collect for Epiphany* I.

# The Lord's Prayer

is our appointed task in the Kingdom whose coming we desire. 'Lord, what wilt thou have me do?'[1] Recognising our responsibility we express our readiness. The great adventure awaits us.

The enterprise of the Kingdom, however, is not such a light-hearted venture, or, in other words, such fun, as some of its more lively modern exponents have represented. The Christian hero, the knight of the Cross, the athlete of the Kingdom, who would 'enter violently,' will do or die. His zeal for the Kingdom of God is inspired by something more than the mere attraction of 'the sporting chance.' In the cause of love he will suffer, if need be, will even accept the great sacrifice, will 'lay down his life for His friends.'[2] And if death does thus come to him, it is a noble death *pro patria*, for the Kingdom of our Father. The world is indeed the poorer for his loss, but the richer for his life and for his sacrifice. He has advanced the Kingdom on earth, and his reward is service in heaven, authority 'over cities.'[3] The will of God has not lost its 'good and faithful servant,'[4] for his valorous efforts, his energies for the Kingdom, are conserved for our emulation, and consummated in higher service. Yet we are not thereby justified in regarding the horrors of

[1] Acts ix. 6.
[2] John xv. 13.
[3] Luke xix. 17.
[4] Matt. xxv. 21.

# The Will of the Father

warfare, for example, or even its splendid sacrifices, as being the Divine Will. Our duty to the dead is to make war impossible by working for the Kingdom of Immanuel. We can only see death as God's will in so far as it is a transition to fuller service. Death is thus 'swallowed up in victory,'[1] accepted with hopeful confidence, not bewailed with the sigh of submission. The petition 'Thy will be done' is ever the prayer of resolute purpose, the assertion of a faith which nothing can daunt. As we 'do the will' we shall 'know the doctrine,'[2] because in our prayers we bring all our hopes and work to God. Our plans for the Kingdom can thus never be merely our own desires, for the Kingdom is the expression of God's own will, teaching, correcting, and, above all, inspiring the wills of men.

The prayers, and indeed the whole life, of our Lord are the truest interpretation of the petition 'Thy will be done, as in heaven, so on earth.' For Christ recognised that the Father's will could only be fulfilled by the founding upon earth of the Kingdom of God. His mission, He declares, is to do the will of His Father. 'I come down from heaven, not to do mine own will, but the will of him that sent me.'[3] Thus St. Paul says of his Master that He 'pleased not himself.'[4] Yet the life of Christ was not one

[1] 1 Cor. xv. 54.  
[2] John vii. 17.  
[3] John vi. 38.  
[4] Rom. xv. 3.

## The Lord's Prayer

long submission. We have already spoken of His zeal for the Kingdom, His joy in its progress, His resolute determination on its behalf. It was indeed His very life. 'My meat is to do the will of him that sent me, and to accomplish his work.'[1] Moreover, the Saviour was never content to see a proof of the Divine Will in suffering. He saw rather its sorrow, and pronounced the will of God to be its remedy. Thus to the question of His disciples, 'Rabbi, who did sin, this man, or his parents, that he should be born blind ?' He answers, 'Neither did this man sin, nor his parents: but that the works of God should be made manifest in him. We must work the works of him that sent me.'[2] In the work of His ministry He does not glorify the hardships of His daily life, but only once refers to them, and that in order to test the faith of a would-be disciple. 'A certain scribe came and said unto him, Master, I will follow thee whithersoever thou goest. And Jesus saith unto him, The foxes have holes, and the birds of the heaven have nests; but the Son of Man hath not where to lay his head.'[3] Further, he foretells His death, not as a foregone conclusion, but as a startling fact, inevitable, not as fate, but as the necessary consequence of man's will, of His people's rejection. Our Lord does not regard His Passion merely as a natural evidence of

[1] John iv. 34.  [2] John ix. 2-4.  [3] Matt. viii. 20.

## The Will of the Father

God's will, but also as the tragic issue of conflicting purposes. If His Father will not overrule the wills of men, then the Son will suffer for mankind. Thus in His Agony He prays, 'Abba, Father, all things are possible unto thee; remove this cup from me: howbeit not what I will, but what thou wilt.'[1] The evil of the cup of suffering is realised, while the power and love of God are affirmed, for even death cannot destroy His faith.

Victory through prayer is the lesson of the Agony. The conflict ended in trustful resolution, in the determination to do the Father's loving will. Our Lord prevailed by prayer because for Him prayer was the expression of His trust in God, His communion with the Father. It was thus that He learned the Father's will, the Divine plans for the Kingdom, and received power for their accomplishment. Nor had He any doubts, as we know from so many of His sayings in the Gospels, with regard to the efficacy of prayer. It is interesting to notice that the Fourth Gospel, when it records that a 'voice from heaven' was heard when our Lord prayed, is careful to add that it was not given as an assurance to Him who prayed, but for the sake of 'the multitude that stood by and heard it.'[2] Such was the confidence of the Saviour, and such His loving

[1] Mark xiv. 36.  [2] John xii. 28-30.

## The Lord's Prayer

obedience, His trust in the Father's will. The 'mystery'[1] of God's will has been revealed in Jesus Christ, and it is for us to claim the privilege of being 'God's fellow-workers,'[2] after the example of His Son. And as we accept our vocation, as we resolve manfully to do the Father's will, we too shall need no voice from heaven to assure us that our prayers are heard, for 'His will is our peace.'[3] Yet the ever-observant multitude will recognise that God has spoken to us, that He is helping us, and that we are working with Him for His Kingdom, His fulfilment of the prayer taught us by His Son, 'Thy will be done, as in heaven, so on earth.'

[1] Eph. i. 9.
[2] 1 Cor. iii. 9.
[3] Dante, *Paradiso*, iii. 85.

CHAPTER VII

## Our Daily Bread

'*Give us this day our daily bread.*'—Matt. vi. 11.

'*In nothing be anxious; but in everything by prayer and supplication with thanksgiving let your requests be made known unto God.*'—Phil. iv. 6.

As we come to consider this clause of the Lord's Prayer we may perhaps feel that there is a certain abruptness in the quick transition from the glory of God to the needs of men. We might have expected that the first petition for man would be a prayer for forgiveness, with an acknowledgment of repentance, in accordance with the command, 'Repent ye; for the kingdom of heaven is at hand.'[1] Yet the fact that this prayer for daily sustenance is put first only further emphasises the essentially practical character of the Kingdom of God. Our Lord, as we know from the Gospels, was accustomed in His preaching and ministry to bring the ideal of the heavenly Kingdom into close association with the earthly wants of His fellow-men, and to show the true relation-

---

[1] Matt. iii. 2, iv. 17, etc.

# The Lord's Prayer

ship between eternal life and the life of every day. We have already noticed that suffering called forth at all times the compassion of the Son of Man, and we can see no less plainly that the struggle for life, the difficulty of satisfying physical necessities, aroused His deep sympathy. As He proclaimed the Kingdom and its requirements, and maintained the duty of man to obey God's loving will, so also at the same time He declared the loving care of the Father for His children in their necessities, 'Your heavenly Father knoweth that ye have need of all these things.'[1]

Moreover, we must also remember that the sight of poverty was familiar to our Lord, who for our sake 'became poor,'[2] and in order that He might preach the Kingdom gave up His livelihood. There can thus be no doubt that He became conversant with poverty and its problems, not as being Himself, in the first instance, desperately poor, for neither His family nor His friends were paupers, but because as the Son of Man nothing of our humanity could be alien to His consideration. Our Lord in His teaching recognises the fact of poverty, 'the poor ye have with you always,'[3] and it is one of the proofs of His Messiahship that 'the poor have the gospel preached unto them.'[4]

[1] Matt. vi. 32.    [2] 2 Cor. viii. 9.
[3] Matt. xxvi. 11.    [4] Matt. xi. 5.

## Our Daily Bread

Yet this does not mean that poverty must be accepted as an unavoidable necessity, but rather that, as in the case of suffering, its existence is a continuous call to effort on behalf of God and His Kingdom. We can see how such a call came to our Lord and what was the response He made. During His forty days of temptation in the wilderness the first suggestion to make use of His Messianic powers came to Him from His physical nature, at the prompting of the pangs of hunger. His zeal to learn the Father's will was so ardent, the power of the Spirit so compelling, that when He sought the undistracted seclusion of the desert He, like His disciples afterwards, 'forgot to take bread.'[1] Yet the temptation to make stones into bread was, we may surely conjecture, prompted by something more than the natural instinct of self-preservation. The Messiah could never, even in the wilderness, be a mere individual. He was Messiah by virtue of His God-given authority over God's own people. And it may well be that, as He hungered, His thoughts were with the hungry and destitute among His fellow-countrymen. The temptation to perform a miracle of feeding would thus be the suggestion not merely that Messiah should find food for Himself, since the fast which He endured was self-assumed and voluntary,

[1] Mark viii. 14.

## The Lord's Prayer

but rather that He should 'prepare a table'[1] in the wilderness for His people, to whom the idea of a Messianic meal was a familiar conception.[2] The question indeed to be decided by our Lord was whether He should not put Himself forward as the avowed champion of the poor, with a definite scheme for the relief of their distress. Such a temptation would have for Him a very powerful attraction.

The suggestion, however, was discarded and the temptation overcome. The Messiah, as He thought out the question in prayer to His Father, came to see that the only right solution was the declaration of the Book of Deuteronomy, 'Man shall not live by bread alone, but by every word that proceedeth out of the mouth of God.'[3] There were, that is to say, other and more vital considerations for the Son of God than the social and material welfare of His people. In the scheme for the salvation of the world the Kingdom of God must stand first and the well-being of man would follow. Thus the thoughts and prayers of our Lord are reflected in the command which He gave to His followers, 'Seek ye first his kingdom, and his righteousness; and all these things shall be added unto you.'[4] The question is one of

---

[1] *Cf.* Pss. xxiii. 5, lxxviii. 19.
[2] *Cf.* Denney, *Jesus and the Gospel*, p. 210.
[3] Deut. viii. 3.      [4] Matt. vi. 33.

## Our Daily Bread

values, of the right proportion, of the true point of view. The Gospel of the Kingdom is not a system of economics, yet we cannot therefore say that it is independent of all economic considerations, or that Christianity has only to concern itself with the individual and his soul, and can give no thought to his external circumstances. If that be so, we make our faith unsocial and our social efforts faithless. 'Holiness, holiness, what do we want with holiness, we haven't got enough to eat,' the cry of the street orator, is not always so absurd or so insincere as we imagine. A society which comfortably acquiesces in the existence of the most heart-rending poverty and yet calls itself Christian is always liable to reproach. In this connection we do well to notice that our Lord when He sent out His apostles was careful to give instructions as to their means of support. They were to eat such things as were provided for them by the faithful, for 'the labourer is worthy of his hire,'[1] of the sustenance which he earns by his work. In making this declaration our Lord, we may be sure, did not mean to confine such a principle of adequate reward for service to the work of proclaiming the Gospel, but rather to imply that the fundamental assumption of all human industry, 'honest work deserves honest wages,' was

[1] Luke x. 7.

## The Lord's Prayer

applicable also to labour expressly performed on God's behalf.

Work, the service of God and man, is thus the crucial test, the one and only justification of our sufficient maintenance. Anxiety and worry as to ways and means are abolished, not in idle dependence upon the favours of *le bon Dieu*, but in the assured confidence that our heavenly Father is a rewarder of those who work faithfully for the furtherance of His Kingdom upon earth. However much we may insist that His children's wants are the Father's care, yet we need to realize that they are ours also, for as one family we pray, 'Give *us* this day our daily bread.' We cannot shelve our responsibility, the society of God must care for its members. 'Bear ye one another's burdens, and so fulfil the law of Christ,' says St. Paul[1]; while he also reminds us that the individual has his obvious duties to the society, 'If a man will not work, neither shall he eat.'[2] The great danger of riches, according to our Lord's teaching, is that they are more often than not a hindrance to service, 'the cares of this world and the deceitfulness of riches'[3] choke the word of the Kingdom. The possession of riches is a grave responsibility and few are equal to such a solemn trust. 'How hardly shall they that have riches enter into the kingdom

[1] Gal. vi. 2.   [2] 2 Thess. iii. 10.   [3] Matt. xiii. 22.

## Our Daily Bread

of God!'[1] To enjoy great wealth is to be tempted, for riches too often prove a distraction, a confusion of the main issue, a dissipation of endeavour. 'For where your treasure is, there will your heart be also.'[2] A divided allegiance is fatal to the Kingdom of heaven.

We can thus see that although we are not told in what words our Lord Himself prayed for His daily sustenance, yet there is much in His teaching and in His own experience that may help us to a right understanding of this petition for our necessities. Hence we are not unduly disturbed by the fact that the adjective which is translated 'daily' in our versions of the Gospels occurs nowhere else in the whole of Greek literature. It is highly probable that the word was coined by a Greek translator in order to give the exact equivalent for the Aramaic expression actually used by our Lord. This desire for accuracy goes some way to prove that the earliest Christians were anxious to preserve as far as possible the exact meaning of each particular phrase in the Lord's Prayer. We cannot, however, be absolutely certain as to what this adjective which we are accustomed to translate as 'daily' really means. The margin of the Revised Version gives the rendering 'for the coming day.' We may thus, it is said, find a liturgical origin for the word, and regard

[1] Mark x. 23.      [2] Matt. vi. 21.

# The Lord's Prayer

it as having been specially constructed in order to render the prayer suitable for either morning or evening use.[1] Yet the expression may quite possibly be independent of such considerations, and may simply mean for the day, without anxiety for the morrow; 'give us the bread of to-day in its day.' This is in accordance with our Lord's command, 'Be not therefore anxious for the morrow: for the morrow will be anxious for itself. Sufficient unto the day is the evil thereof.'[2] Or even if the word means, as is often maintained, 'sufficient,' so that we may translate, 'the bread of our sufficiency,' the sense of the petition is not thereby altered. Bread for the day is presumably sufficient for the day, adequate for our needs, without thought of luxury or excess. It is thus that Agur prays, in the Book of Proverbs, 'Give me neither poverty nor riches; feed me with the bread of my portion: lest I be full, and deny thee, and say, Who is the Lord? or lest I be poor, and steal, and use profanely the name of my God.'[3] If indeed we are to be workmen for the Kingdom we can pray for our sufficient maintenance, 'the bread of our needs.'

We have elsewhere remarked that it is well to interpret scripture by means of scripture before we presume to go further afield in our

[1] *Cp.* Chase, *op. cit.* pp. 44–53.
[2] Matt. vi. 34.   [3] Prov. xxx. 8 f.

## Our Daily Bread

search for explanations, and there is one passage in the Old Testament which can probably give us a good deal of information as to our Lord's meaning in this petition. The giving of the Manna, as recorded in the Book of Exodus, affords many parallels to this prayer for 'the bread of the day.' Thus we read, 'Then said the Lord unto Moses, Behold, I will rain bread from heaven for you; and the people shall go out and gather a day's portion every day, [literally, 'the thing of the day in its day,'] that I may prove them, whether they will walk in my law or no.'[1] Only that quantity of the Manna which was necessary for the day was to be gathered each day, and the command is also given that it must be eaten the same day, and not kept until the morrow. Moreover, the gathering of this miraculously given food was to be regulated by means of a further miracle. It is interesting to notice the exact wording of the narrative, 'And Moses said unto them, It is the bread which the Lord hath given you to eat. This is the thing which the Lord hath commanded, Gather ye of it every man according to his eating; an omer a head, according to the number of your persons, shall ye take it, every man for them which are in his tent. And the children of Israel did so, and gathered some more, some less. And when

[1] Exod. xvi. 4.

# The Lord's Prayer

they did mete it with an omer, he that gathered much had nothing over, and he that gathered little had no lack; they gathered every man according to his eating. And Moses said, Let no man leave of it until the morning.'[1] The Manna was thus given by God to the Israelites as their 'sufficient bread,' apportioned day by day according to their necessities.

We may here notice as a matter of no small interest that the meaning of the command in Exodus, 'the people shall go out and gather the thing of the day in its day,'[2] was variously explained by the early Jewish commentators. A modern writer on the Gospels has drawn attention to this fact and has emphasised its significance for the exposition of the Lord's Prayer. Thus he says, 'The Jews themselves differed in their interpretations of the passage in Exodus. Rabbi Joshua said that they were to collect from one day to the next as one does from the sabbath-preparation-day to the sabbath itself; Rabbi Eleazar denied this. In a prayer of this kind, " the bread of the day " might have meanings varying with the time of day when it was uttered and with the time from which one reckoned " the day " as beginning, whether at sunrise as in nature, or at midnight as among the moderns, or at sunset as among the Jews. There are good reasons for concluding that,

[1] Exod. xvi. 15–19.      [2] Exod. xvi. 4.

## Our Daily Bread

in the Lord's Prayer, the Greek word that we render "daily" meant "belonging to the day that is now coming on," which would be specially appropriate to a prayer uttered in the early morning. But the conclusion could not easily be reached without studying the ancient precept in Exodus.'[1] If we turn once again to the original narrative in the Old Testament we find the words: 'And in the morning the dew lay round about the camp. And when the dew that lay was gone up, behold upon the face of the wilderness a small round thing, small as the hoar frost on the ground.'[2] The occasion of the giving of the Manna was thus the very early morning, and the command to 'gather the thing of the day in its day' would necessarily refer to the coming day. We may compare the account of the Manna in the Book of Wisdom:

'For that which could not be ignored by fire,
Simply warmed by a faint sunbeam melted away;
To make known that we must rise before the sun to give thee thanks,
And must plead with thee at the dawning of the light.'[3]

Lastly, before leaving our discussion of scriptural evidences, we may record the comment of

[1] E. A. Abbott, *The Law of the New Kingdom*, p. 204.
[2] Exod. xvi. 13 f.  [3] Wisd. xvi. 27 f.

# The Lord's Prayer

Rabbi Eleazar as to the moral of the story of the Manna. 'He that hath what he shall eat to-day, and saith "What shall I eat to-morrow?" is of little faith.'[1]

A detailed study of the miracle of the Manna not only helps us in the elucidation of this petition for our daily needs, but also serves to explain the significance of our Lord's teaching on the subject of 'bread,' whether literal or metaphorical. Thus, to refer once again to the Temptation of our Lord in the wilderness, it would seem certain that the refusal to make stones into bread was the outcome of meditation upon the story of the Manna. The passage which our Lord quoted from the Book of Deuteronomy has, in its original context, a direct reference to the story. 'And thou shalt remember all the way which the Lord thy God hath led thee these forty years in the wilderness, that he might humble thee, to prove thee, to know what was in thine heart, whether thou wouldest keep his commandments or no. And he humbled thee, and suffered thee to hunger, and fed thee with manna, which thou knewest not, neither did thy fathers know; that he might make thee know that man doth not live by bread only, but by every thing that proceedeth out of the mouth of the Lord doth man live.'[2] The Messiah might naturally be

[1] Sotah, 48b.   [2] Deut. viii. 2 f.

## Our Daily Bread

expected to follow the example of Moses and provide food in the desert for the people consigned to His charge, but our Lord remembers the teaching of Deuteronomy as to the true lesson of the Manna. He would shepherd His flock with the words of life rather than feed them by a miracle. Similarly in the discourse which the Fourth Gospel appends to the feeding of the five thousand our Lord says 'Ye seek me because ye ate of the loaves and were filled,'[1] while He contrasts Himself as 'the bread of life,' 'the true bread out of heaven,'[1] with the Manna which the fathers ate in the wilderness and yet died.[2] Hence we might expect that the prayer for daily bread, from its association with the story of the Manna, should have a mystical as well as a literal meaning.

We need, however, to guard against any 'spiritual' interpretation of these words which deprives them of their actual and literal meaning as a prayer for the satisfaction of our material necessities. The petition is not a mere allegory of the soul's need, but rather a parable in prayer. We are right, then, to maintain that it has a sacramental meaning, a higher significance arising out of the lower, remembering that our Lord used to speak of 'bread' in both senses, the literal and the figurative. This was natural to Him, for amongst the Jews of His day every

[1] John vi. 32.      [2] John vi. 35, 41.

# The Lord's Prayer

meal, every 'eating of bread,' was accompanied by an act of worship. A blessing was pronounced over the bread, which always formed the chief constituent of the meal. Hence we find that for the Jew bread assumed an almost sacred character, and that elaborate rules were drawn up by the Rabbis for its treatment at table. We are not surprised, then, that meal-times were often used by Christ as occasions for His teaching. The blessing of the bread would form a fitting introduction to the serious discussion of religion. Though our Lord was known to the scribes and Pharisees as 'he that receiveth sinners and eateth with them,'[1] yet we find that He would accept the invitation of certain of the Pharisees when they asked Him to 'eat bread' with them, and that He discoursed with them at table concerning the Kingdom and its righteousness. Thus we are told by St. Luke that on a sabbath-day He went into the house of a ruler of the Pharisees, and that in reply to the utterance of one of the guests, 'Blessed is he that shall eat bread in the kingdom of God,' referring, doubtless, to prevalent ideas as to the Messianic meal, our Lord spoke the parable of the Great Supper with its lesson of the universal Kingdom of the Father's love.[2] Again, it is natural to suppose that our Lord's miracles of feeding were as much parables as miracles,

[1] Luke xv. 2.     [2] Luke xiv. 15-24.

## Our Daily Bread

in accordance with His great fundamental principle of the Kingdom, elaborated during His forty days of temptation, that man depends for his well-being upon the satisfaction of his spiritual as well as his material wants. Hence, for example, when He took the five loaves and two fishes, and blessed and brake them,[1] we may believe that our Lord used the opportunity to teach His followers the 'mysteries' of the Kingdom, and that He prepared them for the fuller sacramental teaching which He gave at the Last Supper, when He instituted the sacred rite of the Eucharist, 'the bread which we break,' and 'the cup which we bless,' to quote the words of St. Paul.[2]

Thus, although, as St. Paul elsewhere reminds us, 'the kingdom of God is not eating and drinking,'[3] yet this petition for our daily bread is a true prayer of eucharistic fellowship. For it was, we cannot forget, common bread which was taken by our Lord to be the symbol of His body, and the communion of His body and blood was ordained by Him as a sacrament at a meal taken in company with His friends. 'Thus common eating and drinking are touched for the Christian with a sacramental meaning; and the sharing the good things which God provides for our nourishment is one chief means of realising the unity of the Christian body

[1] Mark vi. 41.   [2] 1 Cor. x. 16.   [3] Rom. xiv. 17.

# The Lord's Prayer

which is in the one Spirit. There is no real Christian meal which ought not to be consecrated by the thought of unity with Christ, and lifted by the sense of brotherhood and co-operation. "Give us this day our daily bread," the bread for the body, and through the bread for the body that life of the soul also which is communion with God and with our brother men.'[1] It is in this sense that we can pray not only for the bread of our bodily needs but also for the 'super-substantial' bread, the true bread from heaven, not the Manna which melted away and vanished as soon as the sun was up, but the strong meat, 'the athletic food,' as Origen called it,[2] fit for those who would labour manfully for the Kingdom of God and His Christ.

We may now say that in spite of verbal difficulties of interpretation the main sense of this prayer for our daily bread is clear enough. We are bold to ask for the relief of our necessities, both physical and spiritual. For indeed we can feel no shame that our prayer is a petition, an asking from God, a request that our Father will show His love for His children. Yet the prayer is not mere petition, for as we ask we also gratefully acknowledge that all good gifts are from God. Hence it is that St. Paul says 'In nothing be anxious; but in everything

---

[1] Gore, *Prayer and the Lord's Prayer*, pp. 74 f.
[2] Origen, *De Oratione*, xxvii. 9.

## Our Daily Bread

by prayer and supplication with thanksgiving let your requests be made known unto God.'[1] And with regard to material things, we are not selfish in our requests, for we make petition only in so far as we realise such things to be good for us; we ask 'according to His will.' It is thus a false asceticism which says 'I will use no petitionary prayer, I will ask for nothing, but accept what the Lord sends.' We may surely ask the Father to give His children their desires, if those desires are for what is useful in their work for the Kingdom. God allows men some knowledge of what is for their good, and as we pray we grow in knowledge and come to see what is the greatest good for the family of our Father.

Daily bread, our sufficient maintenance, is thus the gift of God to His children. It is the necessary provision for our daily task, not a regulated reward or a grant in return for services rendered, but the sustenance which is essential to our united work for God. 'They received every man a penny.'[2] Thus it is interesting to notice that St. Clement of Rome, when he writes to the Church of Corinth and praises them for their liberal frugality, says 'Ye were more glad to give than to receive, and were content with the provisions which God supplieth.'[3] The bread of God's family is the bread of each

---

[1] Phil. iv. 6.      [2] Matt. xx. 9
[3] Clement, *Epist. ad Cor.* § 2.

# The Lord's Prayer

man's portion, and it is for us to see that there is no injustice in its distribution—neither selfish monopoly nor ill-considered charity. The early Fathers of the Church made the text, 'It is not meet to take the children's bread and cast it to dogs,'[1] the regulating principle of their benevolence.[2] Thus to pray for our daily and sufficient bread is to pray for social righteousness, that each may have what is properly his own. The Christian social order cannot neglect the interests of any of its component parts, for by so doing it ceases to be Christian. That family which sincerely and honestly studies to secure the true welfare of all its members is the only family which can pray 'Our Father.'

We see, then, how far-reaching are the implications of this petition, how wide is the love of our heavenly Father, how deep is our obligation to do His service. For in this prayer, as we ask our God for our daily bread, we acknowledge that He is the giver of all our good, and we pray that He will grant to each one of us 'the bread of our portion,' the sustenance both of body and soul, which will support us in our daily work, that so each and all may, in the strength of that food, without fear or anxiety, but valiantly and with united effort, assault and capture the heavenly citadel, the stronghold of the Kingdom of God.

[1] Mark vii. 27.   [2] *Cf.* Basil, *Reg. Brev.* 100 f, 298.

CHAPTER VIII

## Forgiveness

'*And forgive us our debts, as we also have forgiven our debtors.*'—Matt. vi. 12.

'*Be ye all likeminded, compassionate, loving as brethren, tenderhearted, humbleminded.*'—1 Peter iii. 8.

*T*HE words of this petition are, apparently, so simple and straightforward that it is customary to regard them as a self-evident axiom of Christian conduct. Yet in thus taking them for granted, it is possible that we may overlook much of their real meaning. We are inclined to forget, for example, that they are not a general maxim from the Sermon on the Mount but a definite petition in the Lord's Prayer, and that they have their own proper place in the ordered sequence of the model for all prayer.

The position, indeed, of this prayer for forgiveness is important, since, as we have already seen, there is a clear purpose and design in the order of petitions which our Lord bids us address to our heavenly Father. Thus we learn that in all prayers to God His holiness must stand first, a holiness to be realised by means of the Kingdom, achieved according to His will by men and among men, and that with this end in view we

# The Lord's Prayer

pray for the relief of our necessities and the forgiveness of our sins. With the vision of the Kingdom before us, with the anxiety of our present needs allayed, we reflect upon the past and recognise our failures. In the Lord's Prayer we do not, as in much of our public worship, first plead our incapacity and our unworthiness, and then proceed to learn the Divine Will.

From this it follows that the desire for service is the inspiration of repentance, and confession the sorrowful acknowledgment of our insufficiency. Thus when the moralists of the day assert that men have no need to worry about their sins, and that the one great requisite is 'to be up and doing,' we reply that it is this very eagerness for action which makes us yearn to be rid of the oppressive burden of our shortcomings, the haunting sense of our futilities. The writer of the Epistle to the Hebrews shows his deep insight into the true nature of sin and of man's desire for forgiveness when he says 'Therefore let us also, seeing we are compassed about with so great a cloud of witnesses,'—seeing, that is to say, that we have before us the examples of so many daring heroes of the faith,—' lay aside all encumbrance, and the sin which doth so closely cling to us, and let us run with patience the race that is set before us, looking unto Jesus the captain and perfecter

# Forgiveness

of our faith.'[1] It is, indeed, the grand endeavour of the Kingdom which sets men seriously to think about their sins.

This petition, therefore, for release, involves a candid recognition of the actual existence of sin. We do not pray that God in His omniscience will decline to notice that which we ourselves are disposed to consider as imaginary, but rather that He will forgive what is for us a hard, persistent, and, it would almost seem, irrevocable fact,—our infinite indebtedness. 'If we say that we have no sin, we deceive ourselves, and the truth is not in us,'[2] and 'If we say that we have not sinned, we make him a liar, and his word is not in us.'[3] Hence it is that we approach our heavenly Father with frank acknowledgment of our failures, for we realise 'every man his own plague and his own sorrow,'[4] and we pray, as the Book of Chronicles tells us that Solomon prayed, 'Hear thou from thy dwelling place, even from heaven; and when thou hearest, forgive.'[5]

Moreover, as we pray 'Forgive us,' we acknowledge that sin is not only individual but social. The family has failed, and it is our fault. 'We are members one of another,' says St. Paul,[6] and if one member sins, it is obvious

---

[1] Heb. xii. 1-2 (R.V. marg.). [2] 1 John i. 8.
[3] 1 John i. 10. [4] 2 Chron. vi. 29.
[5] 2 Chron. vi. 21. [6] Eph. iv. 25.

## The Lord's Prayer

that the others are affected. The results of man's sin are often, no doubt, to be seen in himself, but they are more plainly evident in the body corporate. They are 'writ large' in the failures of society. The poignancy of his contrition is the thought that by sin he has forfeited his place in the Father's household; 'I am no more worthy to be called thy son.'[1] He has been false to the high tradition of God's family, and has failed to discharge the obligations of his nobility. Sin is thus man's insolvency, his inability to pay the debt of love which he owes to God in the service of his fellow-men. Yet he does not despair, for, as he acknowledges, God is still his Father, and even if 'our heart condemn us, God is greater than our heart, and knoweth all things.'[2]

There can indeed be no despair for the soul which repents, which resolves, that is to say, no longer to fritter away energy upon mere selfish gratification, but to return to the busy family of God. The Prodigal felt himself to have sinned grievously: his conduct, as the elder brother complained, had been reprehensible to the last degree, yet, in spite of everything, he determined to go back to his father and to offer such service as he might still render, if not as a son, then, at least, as a 'hired servant.'[3] Our Lord Himself, as we read in the Gospels, accepted

[1] Luke xv. 21.   [2] 1 John iii. 20.   [3] Luke xv. 19.

## Forgiveness

the ministrations of a woman 'which was a sinner,' with the words 'Her sins, which are many, are forgiven; for she loved much.'[1] Her expression of humble, loving service, as she wept, not in helpless sorrow, but using her very tears to wash the Master's feet, gave sure proof of her sincere repentance.

Love is thus the fruit of forgiveness, and service the gratitude of the forgiven. 'He to whom little is forgiven, the same loveth little.'[2] Is man therefore to presume upon God's mercy and to put no check upon his sins in order that he may accumulate the benefits of Divine forgiveness? or, in St. Paul's words, 'Shall we continue in sin that grace may abound?'[3] The answer is plain, 'Being now made free from sin, and become servants unto God, ye have your fruit unto sanctification, and the end eternal life.'[4] Yet the remembrance of sin and its forgiveness will make us more forgiving in our behaviour to others, more 'tenderhearted' and more 'humbleminded,' as St. Peter exhorts us.[5] It was to this universal fact of sin with its demands upon our compassion, our fellow-feeling, that our Lord appealed when He saved from death by stoning the woman taken in adultery. 'He that is without sin

---

[1] Luke vii. 37–50.     [2] Luke vii. 47.
[3] Rom. vi. 1.     [4] Rom. vi. 22.
[5] 1 Pet. iii. 8.

## The Lord's Prayer

amongst you, let him first cast a stone at her.'[1]

Sin, we have said, impairs man's capacity for the service of God, and the repentant sinner will find many difficulties in his path. Not only do his old sinful habits endeavour once again to assert themselves, but his fellow-men are not always ready to show that spirit of forbearing love which is demanded of them. Thus there will often be the elder brother to quote the past and to consider himself aggrieved because the sinner has been taken back with joy to the Father's family, while the Pharisee will complain that the Master who accepts the services of such sinners is no prophet, no true judge of character, as he will say. There is not always joy 'as in heaven, so on earth' over the sinner that repents. Yet love will surmount all obstacles in its impetuous onslaught upon the Kingdom, and our Lord warned the stern legalists of His day who had despised the Baptist and his mission of repentance that the publicans and harlots who had repented at the preaching of John were passing into the Kingdom of heaven before their critics.[2]

Our Lord, then, bids us pray that we may be forgiven inasmuch as we also have forgiven. And our forgiveness is tested not merely by our attitude towards sinners in general, but

[1] John viii. 7.   [2] Matt. xxi. 31.

## Forgiveness

by our treatment of those who have sinned against us, of 'everyone who is indebted to us,' as St. Luke renders the petition.[1] Thus in the Gospel of St. Mark the command is given: 'And whensoever ye stand praying, forgive, if ye have aught against anyone, that your Father also which is in heaven may forgive you your trespasses.'[2] Forgiveness is easier as a moral outlook than as a personal virtue, yet we are bidden to forgive our brother no less than our brethren. To exercise forgiveness is usually considered to be the special duty of a Christian, though too often with the proviso that proper allowance is made for the feelings of 'natural resentment.' Yet the law of love allows of no exceptions; if a man will not show the spirit of love by his forgiveness of others, he has no place in the Kingdom of love for which he prays.

It is not necessary to discuss at length the significance of the words 'as we also,' for it is obvious that no question of exact proportion is involved. The extent of God's mercy is not conditioned by the degree of our forgiveness of others. Human forgiveness is, rather, a parable of the Divine. If we forgive, then *a fortiori* God will forgive. The true ratio between our love and God's is that which is expressed in the saying of our Lord, 'If ye then, being evil,

[1] Luke xi. 4.      [2] Mark xi. 25.

# The Lord's Prayer

know how to give good gifts unto your children, how much more shall your Father which is in heaven give good things to them that ask him?'[1]

The obligation of forgiveness was almost unknown to the Gentile world. In Pagan ethics it was noble to show resentment, and to be merciful was to be mean-spirited. The magnanimous man might scorn to notice petty insults, but he forfeited his high soul if he submitted to deliberate injury. In the writings of the Old Testament, on the other hand, we can recognise a growing insistence upon forgiveness as a duty. The *lex talionis*, though never abrogated, received considerable modifications. Thus in the Book of Exodus we read, 'If thou meet thine enemy's ox or his ass going astray, thou shalt surely bring it back to him again. If thou see the ass of him that hateth thee lying under his burden, and wouldest forbear to help him, thou shalt surely help with him.'[2] So also in the Book of Proverbs it is ordered, 'If he that hateth thee be hungry, give him bread to eat; and if he be thirsty, give him water to drink'[3]; and again, 'Rejoice not when thine enemy falleth, and let not thine heart be glad when he is overthrown.'[4]

Further, it is interesting to notice that the

---

[1] Matt. vii. 11.  
[2] Exod. xxiii. 4 f.  
[3] Prov. xxv. 21.  
[4] Prov. xxiv. 17.

# Forgiveness

institution of the Sabbatical year is described in Jewish legislation as 'the Lord's release' in the command, 'At the end of every seven years thou shalt make a release. And this is the manner of the release: every creditor shall release that which he hath lent unto his neighbour; he shall not exact it of his neighbour and his brother; because the Lord's release hath been proclaimed.'[1] Thus the Jewish law intended that there should be a periodical 'remission of debts,' in the literal sense, as a corrective of poverty and an encouragement of brotherly feeling. It is quite possible that our Lord had this passage of Deuteronomy in mind when He bade His followers pray 'release us from our debts, as we also have released those who are indebted to us.' We may recall His sermon in the synagogue at Nazareth when He expounded the passage from the Book of Isaiah with regard to 'the acceptable year of the Lord.'[2]

It is, however, in the Apocrypha and other Jewish uncanonical writings that the duty of forgiveness receives its clearest emphasis. Thus in Ecclesiasticus we read: 'Forgive thy neighbour the injury he has done to thee, and then, when thou prayest, thy sins will be forgiven.'[3] The Testaments of the Twelve Patriarchs[4] has a most interesting passage on the subject

[1] Deut. xv. 1–2.
[2] Isa. lxi. 2, Luke iv. 19.
[3] Ecclus. xxviii. 2.
[4] *circa* 109 B.C.

## The Lord's Prayer

of forgiveness, which is worth quoting in full. 'Love ye one another from the heart; and if a man sin against thee, speak peaceably to him, and in thy soul hold not guile; and if he repent and confess, forgive him. But if he deny it, do not get into a passion with him, lest catching the poison from thee he take to swearing, and so thou sin doubly. And though he deny it and yet have a sense of shame when reproved, give over reproving him. For he who denieth may repent so as not again to wrong thee; yea, he may also honour thee, and be at peace with thee. And if he be shameless and persist in his wrong-doing, even so forgive him from the heart, and leave to God the avenging.' The metaphor of debt, it is to be noticed, occurs in another saying,[1] 'Love one another and set not down in account each one of you, evil against his brother.'[2] Thus St. Paul's saying, 'Charity thinketh no evil,' is more literally rendered as 'Love keepeth no ledger account of evil.'[3] Lastly, in the Story of Ahikar and his ungrateful nephew Nadan, which is supposed to underlie the Parable of the Wicked Servant, we have the command, 'If thine enemy meet thee with evil meet him with good.'[4]

It can thus be seen how Jewish morality had been prepared for the doctrines of Christ as

[1] *Test. Gad*, vi. 3–7.  [2] *Test. Zeb.* viii. 5.
[3] 1 Cor. xiii. 5.  [4] *Story of Ahikar*, ii. 20 (Syr.).

# Forgiveness

to the universal obligation of forgiveness. Our Lord declared that man's mercy must be as unlimited as the Divine. Yet he also maintained, even more emphatically than the Jewish teaching from which we have quoted, that true forgiveness is neither unreasoned nor unconditioned. Repentance, the desire for reconciliation, is essential to all forgiveness, whether by man or God. 'Take heed to yourselves: if thy brother sin, rebuke him; and if he repent, forgive him. And if he sin against thee seven times in the day, and seven times turn again to thee, saying, I repent; thou shalt forgive him.'[1] Forgiveness, when it is exercised promiscuously, may simply result in a benevolent apathy as to our neighbours' conduct, and thus defeat its true purpose, the active release of God's family for God's service.

At the same time there are many cases in which the question of repentance does not arise. Thus the command is given, 'I say unto you, Love your enemies, do good to them that hate you, bless them that curse you.'[2] It is not always remembered, however, that there is a further precept added, 'Pray for them that despitefully use you.'[3] Hence we may, in a spirit of perfect charity with all men, pray that those who inflict injury upon us, whether they be our own personal enemies, or, for example,

[1] Luke xvii. 3 f.   [2] Luke vi. 27 f.   [3] *Ibid.*

# The Lord's Prayer

the foes of our country, may repent, may cease from their despiteful treatment both of our friends and of ourselves, as they come to know God's will, and to realise that it is not by injuring us that they do God's service. The prayer of our Lord on the Cross for His enemies was, 'Father, forgive them, for they know not what they do.'[1] It would seem certain that no one ever sins in full knowledge. Thus by our attitude towards our enemies we do not condone in others the sin which in ourselves we should refuse to tolerate, but in all humility, recognising our own ignorance, we pray that those who do us wrong may learn the error of their ways, and desire to be reconciled with those whom they have injured. The Lord's Prayer is thus more than a general aspiration for the Kingdom of peace; it is a prayer 'appointed to be used in time of war,' a petition that God's divided household may be reunited by mutual repentance and forgiveness.

Our Lord, it is needless to say, did not require to pray this petition for the Divine forgiveness. Yet His compassion for men in their struggles and their failures made Him the friend of sinners. He loved them and, we may be sure, prayed for them that they might repent and be forgiven. 'We have not a high-priest that cannot be touched with the feeling of our infirmities.'[2]

[1] Luke xxiii. 34.     [2] Heb. iv. 15.

## Forgiveness

Thus He knew that many even of the worst sinners, those who most need forgiveness, have themselves something to forgive, the sins of their fathers in a vicious heredity, or the sins of their brethren in a degrading environment. 'It must needs be that offences come: but woe to that man by whom the offence cometh.'[1] If the sinner, in spite of every 'cause of stumbling,' turn once again to his heavenly Father as he sees that even for him there is still some task to be done in the service of the Kingdom, he will forget his grievances, will acknowledge his own debts, and be received once again into the household of God. 'Child, be of good cheer, thy sins are forgiven thee.'[2]

It is to be noticed, in conclusion, that the Lord's Prayer provides no theory of forgiveness, no theological definition of atonement. The cry for forgiveness is instinctive and elemental, and does not pause to reason out any precise principle of remission. 'The child who asks his father to forgive him his disobedience does not trouble himself to define the nature of the mental process which his father has gone through before he gives him his fatherly blessing.'[3] Yet this simple prayer for forgiveness has its implications. 'Release us,' we pray, 'from our debts, as we also have

[1] Matt. xviii. 7.   [2] Matt. ix. 2 (R.V. marg.).
[3] J. H. Bernard, *The Prayer of the Kingdom*, p. 57.

## The Lord's Prayer

released those who are indebted to us.' Sin is the failure to pay the debt which we owe both to God and to His children, and forgiveness is our re-admission by God to the family of His love. Thus forgiveness, the restoration of the Divine favour, cannot be an end in itself. We have prayed to God that His Kingdom may come, and it is with the Kingdom in view that we ask God to release us from the burden of our indebtedness. God forgives us not for what we are but for what we try to be; He sees us as 'the sons of the kingdom.'[1] The Kingdom of heaven 'is within' us,[2] because it was first achieved within the heart of Christ, and in the light of His victory we ask God to forgive us our failures and to allow us once again to work for Him in loving co-operation with our fellows. 'Be ye kind one to another, tenderhearted, forgiving one another, even as God also in Christ hath forgiven you.'[3]

[1] Matt. xiii. 38.   [2] Luke xvii. 21.   [3] Eph. iv. 32.

CHAPTER IX

# Protection and Deliverance

*'And bring us not into temptation, but deliver us from the evil.'*—Matt. vi. 13.

*'Be not overcome of evil, but overcome evil with good.'*—Rom. xii. 21.

AFTER the extreme simplicity of the previous clause the difficulty of this petition seems to be the more disturbing. How can God, we ask, the loving and forgiving Father, be supposed to bring his children into temptation. In natural abhorrence from such a suggestion we turn with relief to the statement of St. James, 'Let no man say when he is tempted, I am tempted of God: for God cannot be tempted with evil, and he himself tempteth no man.'[1] It was, no doubt, this same feeling which led some of the early Latin copyists to write in their versions of the Gospels, 'suffer us not to be led into temptation,' or 'lead us not into such temptation as we are not able to bear.' St. Augustine tells us that in his day many people preferred to pray, 'Suffer us not to be led,'[2] when they recited the Lord's

---

[1] Jas. i. 13.
[2] Augustine, *De Sermone Domini* (Migne *P. L.* xxxiv. p. 1282). *Cf.* Cyprian, *De Oratione Domini*, xxv.

# The Lord's Prayer

Prayer, and it is thus highly probable that the Latin versions were influenced by the liturgical language of the day.

There is no need, however, to tamper with the text in order to solve the difficulty of these words. It is only necessary to remember that this prayer for protection is in two parts, and that both must be taken together to determine the meaning of the whole. The duality of the petition, constructed after the regular Hebrew method, not only saves from unworthy thoughts as to the nature of God's guidance, but also prevents any dualistic interpretation, any Manichæan suggestion that there are two elemental and original principles of right and wrong, good and evil, God and the devil, set one against the other. In this petition God and His providence stand first as evidence of the fact that it is by Him in His fatherly care for us that our lives are ordered and directed. This conception, indeed, of God as the providential ruler of the universe was, as we have seen, one of the avenues by which men came to think of Him as Father. God knows what is right and good for His children, and if trials and temptations come, they are for our good, they are allowed by Him, even though they are not originated by Him. We are in His charge as He 'brings' us, rather than leads us,

# Protection and Deliverance

and we feel that 'the hand of our God is upon us.'[1]

It must also be noticed that the word 'temptation' has both a good and a bad meaning, since the Greek term may be translated either as 'temptation' or as 'trial,' in the sense of 'testing.' Hence, in the Old Testament, we read that 'God did tempt Abraham,'[2] as a test of his faith. So also the Epistle of St. James says 'Count it all joy, my brethren, when ye fall into manifold temptations; knowing that the proof of your faith worketh patience. And let patience have its perfect work, that ye may be perfect and entire, lacking in nothing.'[3] Faith is not a cloistered virtue that shuns the battle of the world, and a carefully sheltered piety is inclined to be merely self-regarding. Our Lord Himself was 'in all things made like unto his brethren,' for 'he himself was tempted in that wherein he suffered.'[4]

Yet, on the other hand, the Christian is not intended to court temptation, the warrior of the Kingdom will not unnecessarily invite conflict or resort to arms from sheer love of battle. He must first count the cost, must 'sit down and take counsel'[5] whether the

[1] Ezra viii. 31.  [2] Gen. xxii. 1.  [3] Jas. i. 2–4.
[4] Heb. ii. 17–18.  [5] Luke xiv. 31.

## The Lord's Prayer

conflict is one which he should enter, or whether he has forces enough to meet his adversary. And as he reflects, he will realise his fallibility, and will pray for guidance and protection, no less than for strength and resolution. 'Bring us not into temptation,' but if it be Thy Will that we meet this trial, then 'deliver us from evil.' Our Lord in Gethsemane, while he admitted the good intentions of His disciples, counselled them not to over-estimate their strength. 'Watch ye, and pray that ye enter not into temptation: the spirit indeed is willing, but the flesh is weak.'[1] In the same way, in the Parable of the Sower, He affirms that temptation may be fatal to a superficial enthusiasm. 'Those on the rock are they which, when they have heard, receive the word with joy; and these have no root, which for a while believe, and in time of temptation fall away.'[2]

Our Lord, as He tells us Himself, endured temptation. It has been suggested that for this reason He refused to be addressed by the title 'good.' Yet He overcame temptation and defeated the solicitations of evil. He was 'in all points tempted like as we are, yet without sin.'[3] Thus He anticipated that His disciples would have to meet trial and temptation, and in His prayer of intercession He prays that they may be protected. 'I pray not that thou

[1] Matt. xxvi. 41.   [2] Luke viii. 13.   [3] Heb 15.

## Protection and Deliverance

shouldest take them from the world, but that thou shouldest keep them from the evil.'[1] Yet His own experience of temptation and its power led Him to sympathise with His followers in their temptations, and He would, if God so permitted, spare them the agony of conflict. Thus He taught them to pray, ' Bring us not into temptation,' nevertheless, if it be Thy Will that we be tempted, ' deliver us from evil.' Although, as we read, He was driven by the Spirit into the wilderness to the battle of the great forty days, yet it can be seen that He did not ordinarily welcome trial and temptation. Hence when the Greeks, as the Fourth Gospel tells us, came to Jesus, and the splendid but disquieting vision of a world-wide evangelisation presented itself, He prayed, ' Now is my soul troubled; and what shall I say ? Father, save me from this hour. But for this cause came I unto this hour. Father, glorify thy name.'[2]

There is a passage in the Gospel of St. Luke which is of great value for a right interpretation of this petition in which we pray for protection and deliverance. Our Lord addresses to the disciples the words, ' Ye are they which have continued with me in my temptations; and I appoint unto you a kingdom, even as my Father appointed unto me, that ye may eat and drink at my table in my kingdom; and ye shall sit

[1] John xvii. 15.  [2] John xii. 27 f.

# The Lord's Prayer

on thrones judging the twelves tribes of Israel.' Then he turns to St. Peter, saying 'Simon, Simon, behold Satan asked to have you, that he might sift you as wheat: but I made supplication for thee, that thy faith fail not: and do thou, when once thou hast turned again, stablish thy brethren.' St. Peter answers with the declaration, 'Lord, with thee I am ready to go both to prison and to death,' yet receives the Master's solemn warning, 'I tell thee, Peter, the cock shall not crow this day, until thou shalt thrice deny that thou knowest me.'[1]

This brief narrative, taken from what is, perhaps, the most graphic description in the whole Gospels, St. Luke's account of our Lord's last night with his disciples, is familiarly coloured by its most obvious feature, St. Peter's impetuosity and its rebuke. It contains, however, words of a deeper significance than those addressed to the eager disciple; the sinless Master, it would seem, was grateful for the society of His few faithful companions in the stress of His temptations. And, yet more wonderful, He could foresee and provide against a future trial of faith for one of them. 'When once thou hast turned again,' He says, and by these words assures His follower that the battle had been fought and gained on his behalf. Thus rescued and protected, St. Peter must reflect

[1] Luke xxii. 28–34.

## Protection and Deliverance

His Lord's benevolence; 'stablish thy brethren,' that is, in their temptations. Thus the prayer, 'Bring us not into temptation, but deliver us from the evil,' like the preceding petition, is as much a corporate as an individual request.

It is usual to picture temptation as an attack upon a lonely soul. It was in solitude that Christian met and overcame Apollyon. In single file the saints appear to have passed down the ages doing battle against the forces that would impede their spiritual progress. Alone, too, our Lord faced the tempter in the wilderness; yet it would seem that He did not ordinarily advocate such solitary combat. 'Couldst thou not watch with me one hour?'[1] was His reproach to that very disciple whom He had so lately assured of support in his own trial. Yet St. Peter was not alone to blame; the other disciples also had slept. 'Watch and pray, that ye enter not into temptation,'[2] the words of our Lord's admonition are in the plural. Christ did not say, let each man watch that he enter not, but watch together, strengthening and guarding one another in the bitter hour of trial. The outcome of Gethsemane gave striking evidence that the disciples were not able to stand alone. Forsaking their Master, they had forsaken one another, and St. Peter, in an hour of physical comfort and moral

[1] Mark xiv. 37.     [2] Mark xiv. 38.

# The Lord's Prayer

relaxation, and without the bracing presence of his old comrades, fell an easy prey to the taunts of his new companions, 'Thou also art one of them.'[1]

At this point, perhaps, it is well to remind ourselves what, in accordance with our Lord's teaching, are the chief temptations to which man is liable. There is first and foremost, as He would have us learn from His own temptation, the danger of living 'by bread alone,'[2] the temptation of materialism. In close relation to this is His denunciation of 'the deceitfulness of riches,'[3] and His warning as to undue anxiety concerning 'the things of the morrow.'[4] Riches and poverty, with their attendant cares, may both prove distractions, temptations to divert our energies. Hence He bids us pray, 'Give us day by day our sufficient bread.' Again, there is the danger of tempting God, of expecting Him to do our work for us and to achieve the Kingdom by means of miracles while we stand by as gratified spectators. It was thus that Israel tempted God in the desert at Massah and Meribah,[5] and it was thus that they tempted His Son when they asked for signs and wonders.[6] The only sign to be given them, our Lord declared,

[1] Luke xxii. 58.
[3] Matt. xiii. 22.
[5] Exod. xvii. 7.
[2] Matt. iv. 4.
[4] Matt. vi. 34.
[6] Mark viii. 11.

## Protection and Deliverance

was the sign of Jonah the prophet, at whose preaching the Ninevites repented.[1] Therefore He commands, 'When ye pray, say, Forgive us our trespasses.' Lastly, there is the temptation to seek to do God's work by unworthy methods, to do evil that good, as we hope, may come. This, our Lord shows us, is the most subtle of all the tempter's enticements, the suggestion that in seeking first our own success we may promote the glory of God. Our Lord throughout His ministry had constantly to meet this temptation. Thus He declined the kingship which was offered Him by the enthusiastic multitudes,[2] He refused to listen to His family and friends in their anxious solicitude for His safety,[3] while to the loving remonstrance of the disciple who would turn Him from the path of suffering and death He addressed the indignant rebuke, 'Get thee behind me, Satan, for thou mindest not the things of God but the things of men.'[4] The question at issue was the salvation of the world, not the peril of the Master. 'For what doth it profit a man to gain the whole world, and forfeit his soul?'[5] Hence, instructed by the teaching of the Saviour, we pray, 'Bring us not into the temptation of self-seeking and

[1] Matt. xvi. 4.
[2] John vi. 15.
[3] Mark iii. 31–35.
[4] Mark viii. 33.
[5] Mark vii. 36.

# The Lord's Prayer

self-assertion, but deliver us from the evil of ourselves.'

There is one aspect of temptation as presented in the Gospels which has not yet been discussed. The word 'temptation' is sometimes used as equivalent to 'tribulation,' or 'persecution,' and in this sense seems to be connected with the teaching of our Lord as to the 'end of the age.'[1] Thus it is to be noticed that the same warning, 'Watch, therefore,' is given both with regard to temptation in the ordinary sense[2] and also in connection with the special trials which are to be the 'signs' of 'the end'[3]; in fact, the troubles of the last days seem to be represented as the great temptation. 'Then shall many stumble.'[4] Further, the same perseverance is required in meeting the tribulations of the last great temptation as in meeting the trials of daily life. 'He that endureth to the end, the same shall be saved.'[5] Hence it is quite probable that the earliest Christians would pray the words, 'Bring us not into temptation,' with special reference to persecution regarded as a prelude to 'the end of all things' which, as they believed, was 'at hand.'[6] The Epistle of St. Peter speaks of those who were being 'put to grief

---

[1] Matt. xxiv. 3.
[2] Mark xiv. 34, etc.
[3] Matt. xxiv. 42.
[4] Matt. xxiv. 10.
[5] Matt. xxiv. 13.
[6] 1 Pet. iv. 7.

## Protection and Deliverance

in manifold temptations,'[1] and declares that 'the devil, as a roaring lion, walketh about, seeking whom he may devour.'[2] Again, the author of the Apocalypse, in his message to the Church at Philadelphia, seems to refer to persecution when he speaks of 'the hour of trial, that hour which is to come upon the whole earth.'[3]

It is quite possible, indeed, that the entire petition was used by the primitive Church, in certain quarters at any rate, as a prayer against persecution. The supplication for deliverance from 'the evil' would thus be regarded as a request for preservation from the persecuting power, whether it were the malevolent opposition of the Jews or the official persecution of the Roman authorities. The Apocalypse shows that Satan had become a synonym for the Emperor and his worship by its reference to the martyrdom of Antipas, 'who was killed among you, where Satan dwelleth,'[4] namely, at the temple of the Emperor. Hence it may be conjectured that St. Luke omitted this clause as liable to be perverted into a prayer for deliverance from the diabolical iniquities of the Roman government. For further evidence, however, in support of such a theory the reader must be referred

[1] 1 Pet. i. 6.
[2] 1 Pet. v. 8.
[3] Rev. iii. 10.
[4] Rev. ii. 13.

# The Lord's Prayer

to a later chapter in this volume. It is sufficient here to say that the petition, 'Bring us not into temptation, but deliver us from the evil,' is at all times a prayer for the safety of God's household. 'Grant, O Lord, we beseech thee, that the course of this world may be so peaceably ordered by thy governance, that thy Church may joyfully serve thee in all godly quietness.'[1]

In any discussion of the clause 'deliver us from evil,' it is usually thought necessary to treat at some length the question as to whether we pray for deliverance from 'the evil,' or from 'the evil one.' Scholars are indeed still divided as to which is the more correct rendering of the Greek term. It is quite likely, however, that the expression was intended to be inclusive, a wide generalisation of the evil element in life. Thus in the Gospels 'evil' and 'the devil' are not always synonymous, for our Lord tells us that 'the evil man out of the evil treasure of his heart bringeth forth evil things,'[2] and that 'from within, out of the heart of men, evil thoughts proceed.'[3] Hence we are not committed to a belief in the existence of a personal devil every time we say the Lord's Prayer. Such a belief is neither to be maintained as a necessary article of the Christian

---
[1] Book of Common Prayer, *Collect for Trinity* V.
[2] Matt. xii. 35.   [3] Matt. xv. 19.

## Protection and Deliverance

faith, nor to be decried as a ground fallacy which renders negligible all Christian theology. The words of this clause merely declare the fact of evil and of man's need for deliverance; they make no pronouncement either as to the origin of evil or as to the form in which it presents itself.

The words of the Lord's Prayer cannot therefore be used either as an argument in favour of the existence of a personal devil or as a reason for repudiating such an idea. Yet as we pray to be delivered from 'the evil,' we may well guard against any theory which, by its undue eagerness to personify evil, creates a devil who is nothing less than the anti-God of the Manichæan, or, by representing him as entirely extraneous to ourselves, tends to lessen our responsibility. If, as it seems, the evil in this world of ours can only be fully accounted for as emanating from a superhuman spirit of evil, there is nevertheless ample evidence of wrongdoing which is plainly the outcome of man's evil will. To realise that evil is, in large degree, within us is, possibly, to take our sins more seriously to heart. 'The serpent beguiled me' becomes less attractive as an excuse. Thus when, for example, we say that 'the devil walks our streets,' we remember also that it is our sin and our failure which thus parades itself before our eyes. To diagnose the disease as, in large

# The Lord's Prayer

measure at least, human is to suggest that there may be also a human remedy. Man's necessity is not only God's opportunity but a call upon our energies as well.

Hence for those who pray 'Thy will be done,' who seek to know and to do God's will and to work for His Kingdom, there can be no shelving of responsibility, no careless indifference, whether of complacency or despair. The family of God, with their Father's help, will work out their salvation. The welfare of the Kingdom is the good of each; and to be selfish is to be disloyal. Evil, whatever its origin, is thus 'the wrong good,' and the duty of man is plain, to assert the will of God, to maintain the uniformity of God's loving purpose for mankind against the multiplicity of false interpretations, the myriad divergencies of man's pre-occupations. Thus the great family prayer rightly concludes with a petition against selfishness. 'Bring us not into the temptation of self-deception and self-absorption, but deliver us from the evil of a selfish will.'

CHAPTER X

## Thanksgiving

'*For thine is the kingdom, the power, and the glory, for ever and ever. Amen.*'

'*Thanks be to God, which giveth us the victory through our Lord Jesus Christ.*'—1 Cor. xv. 57.

*T*HE doxology is the voice of the Church, not the precept of the Master. The last petition of the Lord's Prayer seems to leave the disciple in the midst of the fray, striving manfully and hopefully in the stern and continued conflict of good and evil. For indeed the contest can have but one issue, the establishment of God's Kingdom upon earth. Yet in the thanksgiving which the earliest Christians appended to the Prayer taught by their Lord there is more than a mere prophetic vision of ultimate victory. 'The Lord hath done great things for us already, whereof we rejoice,'[1] and the doxology is a song of triumph, recording the *gesta Dei*, the wonderful works of God. 'Not unto us, not unto us, O Lord, but unto thy name give the praise; for thy loving mercy and for thy truth's sake.'[2] There is no need to search for signs and evidences of the Kingdom. 'Wherefore

Ps. cxxvi. 3.   Ps. cxv. 1.

# The Lord's Prayer

shall the heathen say: Where is now their God? As for our God, He is in heaven: He hath done whatsoever pleased Him.'[1] Thus the disciple enters into the joy of his Lord as he thanks the Father of heaven and earth for the revelation of the Kingdom and the manifestation of His Will. 'Even so, Father, for so it was well pleasing in thy sight,'[2] while he joins in the song of the angels, 'Glory to God in the highest, and on earth peace among men of his good pleasure.'[3]

As soon as the recitation of the Lord's Prayer became a recognised part of the public worship of the Christian Church it was natural to conclude the Prayer with an ascription of praise. Jewish prayers usually ended with a formula of either benediction or thanksgiving. The prayer of David, as recorded in the Book of Chronicles, when he made preparation for the building of the Temple and the inauguration of its worship, contains a doxology in which both these elements are combined. 'Blessed be thou, O Lord, the God of Israel our father, for ever and ever. Thine, O Lord, is the greatness, and the power, and the glory, and the victory, and the majesty.'[4] It is noticeable that the doxology to the Lord's Prayer, in all the various forms in which it is found, is an

---

[1] Ps. cxv. 2–3.  
[2] Matt. xi. 26, Luke x. 21.  
[3] Luke ii. 14.  
[4] 1 Chron. xxix. 10 f.

## Thanksgiving

abridgment of the second half of this passage. The Didache, or Teaching of the Twelve Apostles, closes the Prayer with the words, 'For thine is the power and the glory for ever,'[1] while the manuscripts which insert a doxology into the text of St. Matthew agree as to its general form, though they differ as to its exact wording. Thus the Lord's Prayer in the Christian liturgy does not end, as do so many Jewish prayers, with the sentiment, 'Blessed be thou that hearest prayer,'[2] since the invocation 'Father' renders such an affirmation unnecessary, but with the exultant declaration of God's power and majesty as revealed to men.

It is to be noticed that amongst the Jews the solemn offering of thanksgiving to God was essentially a congregational act. Thus the Chronicler records, 'And David said to all the congregation, Now bless the Lord our God. And all the congregation blessed the Lord, the God of their fathers, and bowed down their heads, and worshipped the Lord.'[3] Again, we are told that at the reading of the Law after the return from exile 'Ezra blessed the Lord, the great God. And all the people answered, Amen, Amen, with the lifting up of their hands: and they bowed their heads, and worshipped the

---

[1] *Didache*, § 8. *Cf.* Chase, *op. cit.* p. 168.
[2] Singer, *Authorised Daily Prayer Book*, pp. 55, etc.
[3] 1 Chron. xxix. 20.

# The Lord's Prayer

Lord with their faces to the ground.'[1] Hence it is that the Lord's Prayer is the centre and focus of all our devotions, whether public or private. Even the Eucharist itself is incomplete without the Prayer of thanksgiving for the Kingdom, the Sovereignty of God's Love.

It can thus be seen that the doxology is the natural expression of true and reverent worship. It is the Church's grateful endorsement of the Master's Prayer. As such, it is not only a thanksgiving for deliverance from evil, but a rehearsal of the glorious history of God's dealings with men. 'Now therefore, our God, we thank thee, and praise thy glorious name.'[2] Thus the Father's Name is glorified and exalted, the power of the Divine Will is acknowledged and attested, and the progress of the Kingdom of God and of His Christ is joyfully acclaimed in the paean of God's victors, 'For thine is the Kingdom, the Power, and the Glory. For ever and ever, Amen.'

[1] Neh. viii. 6.   [2] 1 Chron. xxix. 13.

CHAPTER XI

# The Lord's Prayer in St. Luke

IT is too often taken for granted that the shorter form of the Lord's Prayer which is given in St. Luke's Gospel is the more authentic, and that in St. Matthew we have a Hebraic expansion of the original Prayer. Yet brevity is in itself no proof of authenticity, and it may well be that St. Luke, or his informant, purposely abbreviated the Prayer which he received. It is well known that St. Luke, as the Evangelist of the Gentile world, had certain predilections and prejudices, and that his Gospel is in some degree a subjective account, written, that is to say, from his own special point of view.

What, then, were the reasons which led St. Luke to give in his Gospel a shorter version of the Lord's Prayer? They were probably not liturgical, for the longer form is more obviously, by its structure and arrangement, a prayer for public recitation than the shorter. It would seem more natural to suppose that St. Luke recorded a version of the Prayer which he considered to be most suitable to his Gentile readers.

We have already noticed that in the setting which he gives to the Lord's Prayer the Third Evangelist is probably the more correct.[1] Yet

[1] Chapter I. pp. 8 f.

# The Lord's Prayer

however much we admit the extreme probability of the incident with which St. Luke introduces the delivery of the Prayer by our Lord to His disciples, we are not therefore compelled to attribute a similar exactitude to his shorter version of its contents. Nor can we evade the difficulty by supposing that the Lord's Prayer was delivered twice by our Lord, and that on the second occasion He gave a shorter form, which was merely an inexact reminiscence of the Prayer as originally pronounced. In a compact and comprehensive model prayer we may naturally expect some degree of precision as to its wording, and that however often the Prayer was given by our Lord,—for it is probable that the disciples would need to hear it more than once if they were to commit it to memory,—its form would remain practically the same. It is, of course, possible to maintain that St. Matthew's version is the product of fuller reflection on the part of our Lord, yet on a careful examination it must be said that the form of the Prayer which is given by St. Luke has more the appearance of an abbreviation than a rough draft. The reasons for a revision and expansion of the pattern prayer by the Teacher Himself are not by any means so apparent as those which would induce the Evangelist of the Gentiles to give an abridged version of the Prayer.

## The Lord's Prayer in St. Luke

In the title of address to God the simple invocation 'Father' is given, and there is a certain impressiveness in its simplicity. Nevertheless, seeing that our Lord presumably spoke and prayed in the Aramaic language, the word 'Father' can only be a rendering of the customary term 'Abba,' which, as we have remarked, may be translated as 'Father,' 'my Father,' or 'our Father.'[1] It is obvious that a family, no less than an individual, could say 'Abba.' The Pauline and Marcan use of the address, 'Abba, Father,' probably reflects the usage of early Christian worship which preferred to begin the Lord's Prayer with the original invocation, 'Abba.' Hence St. Matthew's version, 'Our Father,' is not only a legitimate but also a more natural rendering of the term, more especially when we remember that the first person plural is used in all the three petitionary clauses of the Prayer.

With regard to the attribute, 'which art in heaven,' the question is, no doubt, more difficult. But here again there is no need to assert that the more Hebraic is the less probable version. Our Lord as a Jew would be naturally inclined to use the language of Jewish worship in so far as it was not at variance with His own teaching. The title, 'Our Father in heaven,' was by no means unknown to the Jews of our

[1] Chapter III. p. 29.

## The Lord's Prayer

Lord's own day, and we never read that Jesus was challenged as to His use of the expression. Hence there is nothing more likely than that our Lord gave to His followers a Prayer in which God was invoked by a name which was by no means foreign to the devotional language of the day. It may thus be inferred that St. Luke omitted the phrase 'which art in heaven' as being, from his point of view, too definitely Jewish in its associations. Elsewhere in his Gospel he will not allow the expressions 'the Father in heaven,' or 'your heavenly Father,' for the reason, doubtless, that heathen readers might suppose that God was only to be found in supra-terrestrial regions. In St. Luke the angels are the inhabitants of the heavenly places, and God is not confined to a Christian Olympus.

The most serious, however, of St. Luke's abbreviations of the Lord's Prayer is his omission of the clause 'Thy will be done.' It is frequently asserted that these words are merely a paraphrase by the First Evangelist of the petition 'Thy Kingdom come.' Yet in view of the fact that our Lord Himself prayed the words in His own prayers,[1] such an explanation is by no means satisfactory. There is no question

---

[1] St. Luke seems to have known of the existence of the clause, because for St. Mark's 'Not what I will, but what thou wilt' in the Prayer of Gethsemane (Mark xiv. 36) he gives 'Not my will, but thine, be done' (Luke xxii. 42).

## The Lord's Prayer in St. Luke

here of the omission of some single word of secondary meaning, but of a whole clause which is essential to the entire meaning of the Prayer, as interpreting its aspirations and petitions according to the true spirit of prayer, 'If we ask anything according to his will, he heareth us.'[1]

St. Luke, then, or the guarantor of his information, the 'eye-witness' whom he consulted, must have omitted the clause for some good reason. It has already been said that there is a very strong subjective element in the composition of the Third Gospel. This does not necessarily mean that St. Luke as a missionary was so intensely absorbed in the propagation of the Gospel that he neglected its ethical content, so that while he recorded the words 'Thy kingdom come,' he would not add 'Thy will be done.' Such a solution of the problem is neither worthy of the Evangelist nor adequate as an explanation of the facts, yet it seems to point the way towards the right answer to a question of great difficulty.

The first days of the Church were not in all respects a golden age. Even the glamour which the Acts of the Apostles casts upon them cannot conceal the existence of bitter controversy, of faction and disunion. The cause of the quarrel was the vexed question as to how far

[1] 1 John v. 14.

# The Lord's Prayer

obedience to the Mosaic law was binding upon Gentile converts to the faith. In the Epistle of St. Paul to the Galatians we can see the degree of violence to which the controversy attained. St. Paul stoutly resisted all attacks upon 'our liberty which we have in Christ Jesus.'[1] The claims of the Judaisers were represented by him as deadening to the active life of the young Church. Thus he asks of his readers, 'This only would I learn from you, Received ye the Spirit by works of the law, or by the message of faith?'[2] while he sums up the whole point at issue with the words, 'If righteousness is through the law, then Christ died for nought.'[3]

Hence it is not unnatural that the crisis should have been reflected in the actual transmission of the Gospel. If in certain quarters the ethical requirements of the Kingdom were wrongly interpreted, St. Luke might be pardoned for omitting expressions that seemed to him ambiguous or had become an occasion for controversy.

Thus it is a matter of some significance that the word 'righteousness' never occurs in the Third Gospel except in the hymn of Zacharias.[4] Hence the saying of our Lord, 'Seek ye first the kingdom of God, and his

[1] Gal. ii. 4.  
[2] Gal. iii. 2.  
[3] Gal. ii. 21.  
[4] Luke i. 75.

## The Lord's Prayer in St. Luke

righteousness,'[1] becomes in St. Luke merely 'Seek ye his kingdom,'[2] while the Beatitude, 'Blessed are they which do hunger and thirst after righteousness,'[3] is scarcely to be recognised in the form, 'Blessed are ye that hunger now, for ye shall be filled.'[4]

If therefore it is evident that certain expressions were avoided by St. Luke on account of their Judaistic tendency, we may ask whether his omission of the clause, 'Thy will be done,' was not also due to the same motive. 'To do the will of God' was a thoroughly Jewish expression. Thus in the Psalms we have, 'I delight to do thy will, O God. Yea, thy law is within my heart.'[5] Nor is there any doubt that in New Testament times 'to do God's will,' or 'to know God's will,' was synonymous with 'to keep the law.' Hence St. Paul says of his opponents, 'If thou bearest the name of a Jew, and restest upon the law, and gloriest in God, and knowest his will.'[6] Again, in the Fourth Gospel the author puts into the mouth of 'the Jews' the sentiment, 'We know that God heareth not sinners; but if any man be a worshipper of God, and do his will, him he heareth.'[7] Further, and perhaps

---

[1] Matt. vi. 33.    [2] Luke xii. 31.    [3] Matt. v. 6.
[4] Luke vi. 21.    [5] Ps. xl. 8.
[6] Rom. ii. 18 (R.V. marg. 'the Will').
[7] John ix. 31.

## The Lord's Prayer

this is even more convincing, St. Luke never uses the expression, 'the will of the Father,' which more than once occurs in St. Matthew. Thus the saying, 'Not every one that saith unto me Lord, Lord, shall enter into the kingdom of heaven; but he that doeth the will of my Father which is in heaven,'[1] has no exact parallel in St. Luke,[2] while the declaration, 'Whosoever shall do the will of my Father which is in heaven, he is my brother, and sister, and mother,'[3] is given in the form, 'My mother and my brethren are these which hear the word of God and do it.'[4] Similarly, in the Parable of the Lost Sheep, the moral of the story which is given by St. Matthew as, 'Even so it is not the will of your Father which is in heaven, that one of these little ones should perish,'[5] in St. Luke appears as, 'I say unto you, that even so there shall be joy in heaven over one sinner that repenteth, more than over ninety and nine righteous persons which need no repentance.'[6] It may also be noticed that in this passage the adjective 'righteous' seems to be used in a satirical sense.

The Acts of the Apostles supplies us with further evidence on this point. St. Paul, in the speech which he made 'standing on the

[1] Matt. vii. 21.
[2] *Cf.* Luke vi. 46.
[3] Matt. xii. 50.
[4] Luke xi. 28.
[5] Matt. xviii. 14.
[6] Luke xv. 7.

# The Lord's Prayer in St. Luke

stairs' in the castle at Jerusalem, tells how Ananias, 'a devout man according to the law, well reported of by all the Jews that dwelt there' (in Damascus), in his welcome of the converted persecutor, had said 'The God of our fathers hath appointed thee to know his will, and to see the Righteous One, and to hear a voice from his mouth.'[1]

We are therefore quite justified in suggesting that St. Luke, or the source of information which he employed, purposely omitted the prayer 'Thy will be done' as likely to give rise to misunderstanding. The peace of the Church must not again be disturbed by quarrels as to the righteousness of the Kingdom and the doing of the Will by obedience to the Mosaic Law. Rather than allow the phrase 'Thy will be done' to become a cause of disruption, St. Luke would cut out the offending member from the clauses of the Master's Prayer, and allow the two first aspirations to interpret themselves. Yet the Prayer loses by this curtailment. The request that the Father's will may be performed on earth as in heaven is in some sense the climax of the Prayer, for when the Divine Name has been sanctified in the salvation of His people by the establishment of the Kingdom, then only can it be said that the will of God is done.

[1] Acts xxii. 12, 14.

## The Lord's Prayer

The prayers which our Lord Himself prayed, as they are recorded in the Gospels, show us that for Him the supplication 'Thy will be done' was fundamental to all prayer. Not only in the Agony of Gethsemane are the words used as 'a strong cry,'[1] but even in the thanksgiving for the progress of the Kingdom in the work of His disciples our Lord acknowledges the fulfilment of the Divine Will. 'Even so, Father, for so it seemed good in thy sight,' a statement which both St. Luke and the First Gospel record in precisely the same form.[2] The proclamation and the establishment of the Kingdom is the 'good pleasure' of the Father. Thus it is St. Luke who records the saying 'Fear not, little flock; it is your Father's good pleasure to give you the kingdom,'[3] though he will not allow the same sentiment to be expressed in the words 'Thy will be done.' Again, the hymn of the angels at Christ's birth was 'Glory to God in the highest, and on earth peace among men of his good pleasure.'[4]

If St. Luke found the expression 'Thy will be done' too Hebraic for his Gospel to the Gentiles, it is not surprising that he should also have omitted the supplementary phrase, 'As in heaven, so on earth,' for this is an essential part of the third petition, and would naturally

---

[1] Heb. v. 7.  [2] Matt. xi. 26, Luke x. 21.
[3] Luke xii. 32.  [4] Luke ii. 14.

## The Lord's Prayer in St. Luke

be rejected along with it. Further, if he had already discarded the attribute 'which art in heaven,' it is only to be expected that he should also omit the phrase which correlates heaven and earth as the sphere of the Divine Will. If the words 'who art in the heavens' appeared to be a localising of the Deity, so too the phrase 'as in heaven, so on earth' might seem unworthy as being a spatial definition of the Kingdom which, in the language of the Fourth Gospel, is 'eternal life.'

Moreover, these considerations receive further support from the fact that an early alternative to the prayer 'Thy kingdom come' was the petition, 'Let thy Holy Spirit come upon us and purify us.'[1] It has been suggested that this prayer owes its existence to liturgical usage, to the practice of using the Lord's Prayer at the 'laying on of hands.'[2] It is quite probable that this invocation of the Holy Spirit owes its preservation to the fact that it was adapted to special uses, but its origin may very likely be due to other causes. St. Luke's Gospel is in some sense the first volume of 'the Acts of the Holy Ghost,' in which the activities of the Spirit accompany the progressive evangelisation of the world. The Spirit is the 'dynamic' of the Gospel throughout its pages. Hence it is, perhaps, that St. Luke very rarely uses the

[1] *Cf.* Chase, *op. cit.* p. 25.   [2] *Ibid.* pp. 28–30.

# The Lord's Prayer

noun 'gospel,' but nearly always the verb 'to preach the gospel.' Thus our Lord's sermon in the synagogue is from the text, 'The Spirit of the Lord is upon me, because he anointed me to preach the gospel to the poor.'[1] Again, the phrase 'the gospel of the kingdom' occurs only once in St. Luke, though it is characteristic of St. Matthew. It would thus seem highly probable that the prayer 'Let thy Holy Spirit come upon us and purify us' is a very early variant of the clause 'Thy kingdom come,' which became current in certain quarters, more especially in the West, where St. Luke's was the prevailing version of the Gospel. This 'spiritualisation' of the petition for the coming of the Kingdom is almost Johannine, and is one of many signs of approximation to Johannine thought and expression in St. Luke, seeing that in the Fourth Gospel 'the gospel of the kingdom' has become the advent of 'the Paraclete' and the possession of 'eternal life.'

It must also be noticed that it is in direct connection with prayer that the introduction of the Holy Spirit in St. Luke's Gospel is perhaps most prominent. Thus the section of teaching in which the Lord's Prayer is placed ends with the saying, 'If ye then, being evil, know how to give good gifts unto your children, how much more shall your heavenly Father give the Holy

[1] Luke iv. 18.

## The Lord's Prayer in St. Luke

Spirit to them that ask him?'[1] which is given in St. Matthew as 'How much more shall your Father which is in heaven give good things to them that ask him?'[2] Again, in the introduction to the prayer of thanksgiving which St. Luke records as having been uttered on the return of the Seventy we read, 'In that same hour he rejoiced in the Holy Spirit, and said, I thank thee, O Father.'[3] St. Matthew has simply, 'At that season Jesus answered and said, I thank thee, O Father.'[4] Thus St. Luke represents our Lord as praying, preaching, and working 'in the power of the Spirit.'[5]

Enough has now been said to show how probable it is that St. Luke would reject such an expression as 'Thy will be done, as in heaven, so on earth' from considerations which appeared to him to be of vital importance. If there was any possibility that such a definition of the Kingdom and its righteousness might be misunderstood and misinterpreted in a Judaic sense, then at all costs it must be avoided. Further, even the very idea of the Kingdom might seem to give countenance to a narrow and exclusive view of the Gospel. If this were so, there were men who, rather than lose their Christian liberty, would speak of the Kingdom

[1] Luke xi. 13.
[2] Matt. vii. 11.
[3] Luke x. 21.
[4] Matt. xi. 25.
[5] Luke iv. 14.

# The Lord's Prayer

in other terms, and would pray for its realisation in 'the coming of the Holy Ghost.' The more valid grounds, therefore, which we can find for the exclusion from St. Luke's Gospel of the clause 'Thy will be done,' the more readily do we believe that, in view of its entire aptitude, not to say its radical necessity, to the thought of the whole Prayer, it has always had a place in that Prayer, and that the Gospel of St. Matthew is right when it declares that our Lord bade His followers pray to their heavenly Father, 'Thy will be done, as in heaven, so on earth.'

In the petitions for daily bread and for forgiveness St. Luke's variants are of little importance. The expression 'day by day' which he gives somewhat inaccurately for 'this day' is characteristic both of his Gospel and of the Acts. Again, in rendering 'debts' by the more general word 'sins' he corrects himself in the second half of the clause by saying 'as we also forgive everyone that is indebted to us,'—the expression 'every one that is' being of frequent occurrence in his writings.

In the last petition, however, there is an omission which is of great importance. What reason had St. Luke to reject the prayer, 'Deliver us from the evil'? The phrase, no doubt, was Jewish in its associations, yet there was no point of doctrine or ethics involved in such

## The Lord's Prayer in St. Luke

prayer. A solution of the problem must be sought in other directions.[1]

We have already had occasion to infer that the petition 'Bring us not into temptation' was used with more particular reference to the temptations and trials which were to be the 'signs of the end,' and that the clause for deliverance from 'the evil' came to be understood as a prayer for the safety of the Church in time of persecution.[2] Hence St. Luke may have omitted the clause 'Deliver us from the evil' as liable to be perverted into a special suffrage for deliverance from the persecuting power, namely, the Roman government. The Apocalypse shows how the Emperor and his worship were spoken of as 'Satan,'[3] and there are certain other passages in the New Testament which seem to represent the persecution of the Christians by the Roman authorities as the direct work of the devil. Thus, for example, in the Second Epistle to Timothy, St. Paul declares, with regard to the result of his first trial at Rome, 'I was delivered out of the mouth of the lion. The Lord will deliver me

---

[1] St. Luke in the explanation of the Parable of the Sower substitutes 'the devil' for 'the evil one.' (Contr. Luke viii. 12 with Matt. xiii. 19. Mark has 'Satan,' iv. 15.) If St. Luke merely objected to τοῦ πονηροῦ as being a Jewish expression he might have used a less Hebraic term.

[2] Chapter IX. pp. 132 ff.     [3] Rev. ii. 13.

## The Lord's Prayer

from every evil work, and will save me unto his heavenly kingdom: to whom be glory for ever and ever. Amen.'[1] Here there seems to be a plain allusion to the language of the Lord's Prayer, while the mention of the 'lion' must be considered in conjunction with the saying of the Epistle of St. Peter, 'Be sober, be watchful: your adversary the devil, as a roaring lion, walketh about, seeking whom he may devour: whom withstand stedfast in your faith,'[2] where the reference to persecution is obvious.

It is important also to notice what was St. Luke's own attitude with regard to persecution. In the Acts the courteous and forbearing behaviour of the Roman officials is contrasted with the malignant attacks of the Jews upon the new sect, while in the Gospel Pilate is represented in as favourable a light as possible.

In the predictions of the tribulation which is to come upon the faithful in the last days we can see that St. Luke's account has been influenced by the actual history of the early Church. The prophecies, as he records them, in many of their details are plainly *post eventum*. Thus St. Luke alone mentions the imprisonments[3] which the Christians were to endure, while he lays greater stress than do the other

[1] 2 Tim. iv. 17 f.   [2] 1 Pet. v. 8.   [3] Luke xxi. 12.

# The Lord's Prayer in St. Luke

Synoptists upon the 'apologies' which they were to utter by the inspiration of the Holy Spirit. 'I will give you a mouth and wisdom, which all your adversaries shall not be able to withstand or to gainsay.'[1] No doubt the speeches of St. Stephen and St. Paul were in his mind as he wrote these words. Hence in the Third Gospel persecution is more a fact of history or of present experience than a portent of the Second Coming.[2] St. Luke manifests his conviction that persecution is only transitory and that patient endurance and a wise apologetic will in the end prevail. Thus he declares: 'Not a hair of your head shall perish. In your patience ye shall win your souls.'[3] His general attitude towards the Roman authorities is conciliatory, inasmuch as the Roman Empire was the field for the missionary activities of the Christian Church. No doubt it was natural, especially for a writer of Apocalypse, to speak of the Emperor Nero, for example, as 'the devil,' yet St. Luke carefully avoids any expression which might be considered by the ruling power as provocative, by seeming

---

[1] Luke xxi. 15.
[2] It is perhaps noticeable that in the explanation of the Parable of the Sower where the other two Synoptists give 'when tribulation or persecution ariseth because of the Word' (Matt. xiii. 21, Mark iv. 17), St. Luke has merely 'in time of temptation.'
[3] Luke xxi. 18 f.

## The Lord's Prayer

to assign the 'temptation' or persecution of the Church to direct diabolical agency.

In conclusion, therefore, it may be asserted that the shorter version of the Lord's Prayer which is given us in the Third Gospel is a form adapted to the use of the mission field by an Evangelist who was before all else a missionary.

CHAPTER XII

# Enthusiasm in St. Matthew

*IT* may seem strange to speak of enthusiasm in connection with the First Gospel. To many readers that Gospel appears as the least attractive account of the Christian message. The fact that much of its material is so strongly Judaic in character, and that the background is so obviously Palestinian, serves, perhaps, to make it the least popular of the three Gospels. There is a feeling that a very large portion of the Gospel is of merely antiquarian interest. There seems also to be a lack of vigour and freshness in its pages. The impression can scarcely be avoided that in many passages spontaneity has been sacrificed to literary artifice and the arguments of early Christian apologetic. The reader misses both the fervid activity of St. Mark and the wide and cheerful optimism of St. Luke, and he finds a certain degree of dulness and stagnation in St. Matthew. It may be questioned, however, whether such an impression is not merely the result of an imperfect appreciation of the contents of the Gospel, and of the circumstances under which it was composed.

One of the most prominent features in the First Gospel is the expectation of an early Parousia. The words of our Lord on this subject

# The Lord's Prayer

would seem to have been eagerly taken up, and possibly over-emphasised, in the circle from which that Gospel emanated.

Recent studies on the Synoptic Problem serve to remind us that there is more eschatological colouring in the First Gospel than in the earlier account by St. Mark. It is maintained that this is in reality an accretion, due to the environment amid which the Gospel was produced. If so, we have a further proof that the Parousia was a most powerful influence in the Palestinian church.

But what were the effects of this influence? Is the eager expectation of an almost immediate Parousia to be regarded only as one of the mistaken ideas which are to be found in this Gospel? Was the result of such an expectation altogether harmful, or at any rate stultifying, to the life of the community? Is it true that no sort of organisation, and no system of Christian morality, could be possible until such a belief had passed away? We are often asked to accept a picture of primitive Christianity which gives us an impression that the expectation of the Coming of our Lord over-shadowed, and almost obliterated, all else.

Let us take first the question of morality. In this sphere the Parousia was neither a deadening obstacle, nor a mere stimulant, having no more than a momentary effect. It is not without

## Enthusiasm in St. Matthew

significance that in the First Gospel, which is, in its contents at least, the most eschatological of the three, we have great prominence given to moral teaching, and to the ethical requirements for entrance to the Kingdom of Heaven. And this is not mere 'interim ethics,' in the sense that it is to serve only for the time being. There is a carefulness of reproduction, and a painstaking attention to grouping, which shows that the author was quite serious as to the importance of morality for the Christian life. The strong feelings of hatred which he evinces for the Pharisees seem to make him the more anxious to show that the morality of the Christians does actually exceed that 'of the Scribes and Pharisees.' There is, then, no relaxation of moral requirements in view of the expected Parousia. Nor is there any universal call to the practice of asceticism in anticipation of that event. Self-denial rather than asceticism is the note of Christ's moral teaching in the Gospel of St. Matthew. In St. Paul the fact that 'the time is shortened'[1] seems to be responsible in some degree for his preference for the celibate life, and it is interesting to note that the reference to those who have 'made themselves eunuchs'[2] with a view to entering the Kingdom of Heaven, or for the sake of furthering its cause, is to be found only in the First Gospel, which, as we have

[1] 1 Cor. vii. 29.   [2] Matt. xix. 12.

## The Lord's Prayer

seen, may fairly be called the most eschatological. But even if asceticism in this respect is singled out for praise, it is nowhere made into a precept. So, then, in the Gospel of St. Matthew the influence of eschatological considerations is to be seen in an enthusiastic but orderly morality. And the fact of its orderliness is still further evident when we consider that the carrying out of moral principles is brought into relation with the action of the church—'tell it unto the church: and if he refuse to hear the church also, let him be unto thee as the Gentile and the publican.'[1] The ethic of the Christian is in no sense individualist. So also in the Parable of the Unmerciful Servant, which immediately follows, it is the 'fellow-servants' who are 'exceeding sorry, and came and told unto their lord all that was done.'[2]

This brings us to consider what was the effect of this expectation of the Parousia upon the common life of the community in respect to organisation. No doubt it is true that little attention could be given to details regarding Apostolic succession, if a belief was held that one at least of the Apostles should 'tarry till I come.'[3] Yet this does not mean that no steps were to be taken to regulate the life of the Christians who were gathered together. It is worthy of notice

[1] Matt. xviii. 17.   [2] Matt. xviii. 31.
[3] John xxi. 22, 23.

## Enthusiasm in St. Matthew

that the word 'church' is mentioned only in the First Gospel. It would seem as if some attention to organisation was not incompatible with a lively expectation of an early return of our Lord. There is, surely, no need to suppose textual interpolation in these passages, if any other explanation is forthcoming. Those who are acquainted with the history of the Irvingite movement know well that a belief in an almost immediate Advent may do much to foster the corporate feeling of a religious body. The Gospel of St. Matthew may well be a 'church' Gospel, and, though local in character, what is lost in extent is perhaps made up for by a gain in intensity. There are many signs besides the mention of the word 'church,' that the First Gospel is in some sense an ecclesiastical book. The division of the Gospel into sections seems to have been done with a view to public reading in church. More than one parable recorded only by this Evangelist has a direct bearing upon the problems of the primitive community. There are indications also of an almost pastoral care exercised by the community for its 'little ones.' In view of the great event they are to be kept safe from all harm. The Parable of the Lost Sheep, with its reference to the 'lost sheep of the house of Israel,' is to be contrasted with St. Luke's Parables of the Lost Sheep and the Lost Drachma with their wider reference to publicans

## The Lord's Prayer

and sinners.[1] Again we have to notice in the account of the 'faithful and wise servant' that our Evangelist alone mentions the possible ill-treatment of the 'fellow-servants.'[2] There is, then, a very strong corporate feeling in the Gospel according to St. Matthew. The Christian body is to be kept inviolate, even at the cost of allowing the Tares to exist side by side with the Wheat. No doubt the thought that the Harvest was not far off made such a principle easier of application.[3]

If, then, there was this feeling of solidarity, we cannot be surprised that there was also a certain, perhaps excessive, bitterness against those who remained outside the community. Toleration is very often absent from those in whom enthusiasm is strongest. Hence we are not surprised to find in this Gospel strong denunciations of the Jews, and more especially of the Pharisees, the counter-enthusiasts of the Christians in Palestine.

Further, a corporate feeling must find expression in corporate action and, in the case of a religious community, in corporate worship. Our Lord gave three great commands to His disciples, which should mould from the first the worship of the Church, viz., to pray as He had taught them, to celebrate His Eucharist, and

---

[1] Contrast Matt. xviii. 10–14 with Luke xv. 3–10.
[2] Matt. xxiv. 45–51.     [3] Matt. xiii. 29.

## Enthusiasm in St. Matthew

to bring men to His Baptism. That these commands were obeyed in the early Palestinian church we know both from this Gospel and the Didache. But what is, perhaps, even more significant is that the inspiration for such observance was the remembrance of our Lord's words as to His Coming. The Parousia was brought into connection with all three commands by our Lord Himself, and cannot have been forgotten by the earliest believers, or by those who immediately inherited their traditions.

With regard to the command to pray we find that our Lord more than once combines with it the injunction to 'watch.' And no doubt for the earliest Christians the watching for the Advent was a great incentive to prayer. While the importance of the Vigil has possibly been over-exaggerated, yet it seems to have played a considerable part in the framing of the Church's system of devotions. Further, the model of all prayer contains the clause 'Thy kingdom come,' words which would have a very vivid meaning to those who watched while they prayed.

Secondly, as regards the Eucharist, while the references to the Parousia are, perhaps, less outspoken, the influence of the expectation of that event is quite as noticeable. We may feel sure that St. Paul was not introducing a new thought when he said 'For as often as ye eat this bread, and drink the cup, ye proclaim the Lord's

## The Lord's Prayer

death till he come.'[1] The Eucharist may well have been regarded as a feast which was to be preliminary to the great Feast of the Kingdom, when it should come. Our Lord's words as to His drinking wine 'new with you in my Father's kingdom' would be likely to support such an idea.

Thirdly, as regards our Lord's command to baptize.[2] We are not here concerned with the question of the Trinitarian formula in St. Matthew. The command is there, whatever 'the Name' may have been. As in the case of John's baptism, the fact that the Kingdom was 'at hand' would serve to bring people eagerly to the Christian rite of initiation. There would be a feeling that the unbaptized would not be ready to meet their Lord. This feeling, perhaps, went so far that even the dead were baptized, it would seem, by proxy.[3] The expectation of an early Parousia cannot very well be said to have led to a neglect of all external religious observance, or a distaste for Christian rites. Once again we may be allowed to point to the history of the Irvingite movement for a parallel.

Further, as to the universality of Christ's injunction to baptize. Difficulty is often felt in reconciling this reference to 'all nations' with the tone of the rest of the Gospel. But it is to

---

[1] 1 Cor. xi. 26.      [2] Matt. xxviii. 19.
[3] 1 Cor. xv. 29.

## Enthusiasm in St. Matthew

be remembered that discipleship is required as well as baptism, so that room would be left for instruction in the Law of Moses as a preliminary to Baptism, in accordance with the spirit of this Gospel. Also it is to be noticed that the preaching of the gospel to the nations [1] is to be 'for a testimony,' that is to say, before the end comes. The Coming of the Kingdom was to be a spur to this missionary effort, even though it did not leave time for such evangelisation to be very thorough. Here again we may refer to Irvingism with its 'Great Testimony.' So then we have seen that the expectation of the Parousia served as an inducement to the carrying out of Christ's three great commands.

But this does not mean that there was a lack of devotion to the Person of our Lord Himself. The watching for the Coming was very largely due to a desire to 'see the Lord' in person,[2] while the nearness of the Advent would serve to keep up a high pitch of devotion amongst those who were waiting for the Lord. The communion with Christ which was thus formed on earth was soon to be consummated in heaven. The Parousia was the aim and end of men's hopes and prayers, while it was also an incentive,

---

[1] Matt. xxiv. 14.
[2] *Cf.* Deissmann, *Light from the Ancient East*, pp. 372 ff., on *parousia* as the technical word for the arrival or visit of the Emperor.

## The Lord's Prayer

and not an obstacle, to their devotion. In this way we can, perhaps, partly account for the attention given to the fulfilment of prophecy in this Gospel. It is usual to explain this by the need for anti-Jewish apologetic. No doubt such a consideration does very largely account for the notices of the fulfilment of prophecy which we find in this Gospel, but they may also have had a nobler origin. The desire to 'search the Scriptures' may have been inspired by a devotion to the Person of our Lord quite as much as by the needs of early Christian apologetic. The primitive Church, whether in Palestine or elsewhere, was not primarily a Christian Evidence Society. And in the circle from which the First Gospel would seem to have emanated we find many reasons for supposing that devotion would find expression in such a form. Church life was intense rather than extensive, parochial rather than missionary, contemplative rather than actively busied in evangelisation. The desire to know more about Christ, not only as the Teacher, but also as the Fulfilment of Prophecy, was quite natural in such a community, apart from any controversial requirements. The fact that many of the parallels from prophecy in this Gospel are not a little fanciful is due, perhaps, not merely to their argumentative and Rabbinical character, but also to their devotional origin. The Odes of Solomon show

# Enthusiasm in St. Matthew

us that the devotions of the early Christians might be not only fanciful but grotesque.[1]

From this survey of some of the leading characteristics of the First Gospel we can scarcely avoid the conclusion that the expectation of an almost immediate Parousia, so far from deadening or stultifying the religious life of the community, was rather an incentive towards an enthusiasm of a corporate character.

It cannot be said that morals were neglected, or that the worship of the Church suffered from such expectation. Devotion would seem to have been deepened, while the necessity of evangelisation, 'as a testimony,' was realised.

Yet it may be alleged that this particular Gospel contains parables which show that the Kingdom is essentially a growth rather than a great event or catastrophe. This is true; but it must be remembered that these parables would probably be explained by the first readers of the Gospel in a very different way. In the Parable of the Mustard-seed, for example, the suddenness rather than the gradual character of the growth would doubtless be emphasised in view of 'the shortness of the time.' Again, the reference to the 'birds of the heaven' who come to lodge in the branches of the tree would suggest the apocalyptic visions of the Book of Daniel. In the same way the secret working

[1] See especially Ode xix.

## The Lord's Prayer

of the Leaven, until suddenly the whole lump is found to be leavened, is not entirely inconsistent with the coming of the Kingdom like a thief in the night.[1]

In conclusion, then, we may say that there is no reason for us to neglect the First Gospel on account of an imagined dulness in its pages. On the contrary, the Gospel possesses a great interest as reflecting the fervour and enthusiasm of the community in which it was produced. It is the Gospel of a church—a local church, it may be—but yet a church which was keenly alive. If St. Luke's is the missionary, St. Matthew's is the 'parochial' Gospel, and both have their value, for each reflects in its own way the enthusiasm of early Christianity.

[1] *Cf.* Matt. xxiv. 43.

CHAPTER XIII

# Illustrations from Jewish Sources

## (1) *Our Father which art in Heaven*

'Be bold as a leopard, and light as an eagle, and swift as a gazelle, and strong as a lion to do the will of thy Father which is in heaven.' Rabbi Judah ben Tema, c. A.D. 150.[1]

'On whom have we to lean? On our Father which is in heaven.' Rabbi Eliezer ben Hyrcanus, c. A.D. 90.[2]

'Happy are ye, Israel: before whom do ye purify yourselves? Who purifies you? your Father which is in heaven.' Rabbi Akiba, A.D. 50–135.[3]

'As often as the Israelites directed their hearts towards their Father who is in heaven they were strong.' Rabbi Simeon ben Jochai, disciple of R. Akiba, c. A.D. 130.[4]

'One should not say: I have no inclination for garments of mixed stuffs, swine's flesh, forbidden wedlock; but one should say: I have indeed inclination for such things, but what shall I do when my heavenly Father has forbidden them to me?' Rabbi Eleazar ben Azariah, c. A.D. 100.[5]

[1] Pirke Aboth, v. 23.  
[2] Sotah, ix. 11.  
[3] Yoma, viii. 9.  
[4] Rosh ha-Shana, iii. 8.  
[5] Siphra, 93*d*.

# The Lord's Prayer

'May the prayers and tears of all Israel be accepted before their heavenly Father.' From the Kaddish.[1]

'Our Father, our King! we have sinned before thee.' The opening clause of the Prayer 'Abinu,' a penitential prayer of forty-four petitions, each beginning with the words 'Our Father, our King,' recited during the ten days of penitence at the New Year.[2]

'One is our God; he is our Father; he is our King; he is our Saviour.' Additional Service for Sabbaths.[3]

### (2) *Hallowed be thy name*

'Let all thy actions be to the name of heaven.' Rabbi Jose the priest, c. A.D. 100.[4]

'Every one who profanes the name of heaven in secret, they exact punishment of him openly; the ignorant and the wilful are alike sinners in regard to the profaning of the name.' Rabbi Johanan ben Berokah, c. A.D. 120.[5]

'Any benediction which is without mention of the name is no benediction at all.'[6]

'Our King, our God, make thy name one in thy world, make thy sovereignty absolute (lit. 'one') in thy world, and make absolute

---

[1] Seder Rab Amram, i. 13b.
[2] Singer, *Authorised Daily Prayer Book*, pp. 55–57.
[3] Singer, p. 161.  [4] Pirke Aboth, ii. 16.
[5] *Ibid.* iv. 5.  [6] Berakoth, 40b.

# Illustrations from Jewish Sources

the remembrance of thee in thy world.' From an ancient prayer.[1]

'May his great name be magnified and sanctified in the world which he has created according to his will. May his sovereignty reign.' Ancient version of the Kaddish.[2]

'We will sanctify thy name in the world, even as they sanctify it in the highest heavens.' Kedushah, Morning Service.[3]

*Reader.*—Magnified and sanctified be his great name in the world which he hath created according to his will. May he establish his kingdom during your life and during your days, and during the life of all the house of Israel, even speedily and at a near time, and say ye, Amen.

*Congregation and Reader.*—Let his great name be blessed for ever and to all eternity.

*Reader.*—Blessed, praised and glorified, exalted, extolled and honoured, magnified and lauded be the name of the Holy One, blessed be he; though he be high above all the blessings and hymns, praises and consolations, which are uttered in the world; and say ye, Amen. Kaddish at Morning Service.[4]

[1] Seder Rab Amram, i. 9a.
[2] *Ibid.* i. 3b.
[3] Singer, p. 45.
[4] *Ibid.* p. 37.

# The Lord's Prayer

## (3) *Thy Kingdom come*

'Then shall God alone be absolute in all the world, and his sovereignty will endure for ever and ever.' Joshua ben Khananya, c. A.D. 100.[1]

'Take upon you the yoke of the sovereignty of heaven.'[2]

'Any benediction that is without the sovereignty is no benediction at all.'[3]

'They shall delight in thy sovereignty, every one of those that keep the Sabbath day; they shall all be satisfied and refreshed in thy goodness.' From an ancient prayer.[4]

'And may he set up his sovereignty in your lifetime, and in your days, and in the lifetime of the whole house of Israel, yea speedily, and in a time that is near.' From the Kaddish.[5]

'May our eyes see thy royal sovereignty.' From an ancient prayer.[6]

'Restore our judges as at the first and our counsellors as at the beginning; remove from us grief and suffering; reign thou over us, O Lord, thou alone in lovingkindness and tender mercy, and justify us in judgment. Blessed art thou, O Lord the King, who lovest righteousness and judgment.' The eleventh petition of the 'Eighteen Blessings.'[7]

[1] Mechilta, 56a.  [2] Siphri, 91b.
[3] Berakoth, 40b.  [4] Seder Rab Amram, i. 29b.
[5] Ibid. i. 3b.  [6] Ibid. i. 10b.  [7] Singer, p. 48.

# Illustrations from Jewish Sources

'And may his kingdom be soon revealed and made visible unto us, and may he be gracious unto our remnant and unto the remnant of his people, the house of Israel, granting them grace, kindness, mercy, and favour; and let us say, Amen.' Morning Service.[1]

## (4) *Thy will be done, as in heaven, so on earth*

'Be ... strong as a lion to do the will of thy Father which is in heaven.' Rabbi Judah ben Tema, c. A.D. 150.[2]

'Make his will as thy will that he may make thy will as his will; efface thy will before his will that he may efface the will of others before thy will.' Rabban Gamaliel, iii. c. A.D. 210.[3]

'Why art thou scourged? because I have done the will of my heavenly Father.' Rabbi Nathan, c. A.D. 160.[4]

'It is our will to do thy will.'[5]

'If any one keeps the law and does the will of his Father who is in heaven.'[6]

'Do thy will in heaven above, and give rest of spirit to them that fear thee beneath.'[7]

'May it be thy will, O Lord our God, to establish peace in the upper family and in the lower family.'[8]

---

[1] Singer, p. 67.
[2] Pirke Aboth, v. 23.
[3] *Ibid.* iv. 2.
[4] Wayyikra Rabbah, 32.
[5] Berakoth, 16b.
[6] Siphri, 872.
[7] Berakoth, 29b.
[8] *Ibid.* 17a.

# The Lord's Prayer

'If a man sanctifies himself below, they sanctify him above.'[1]

'May it be the will of our Father who is in heaven to establish the Temple, the house of our life, and to restore his divine presence in our midst, speedily in our days; and let us say, Amen.' Morning Service.[2]

'May it be the will of our Father who is in heaven to have mercy upon us and upon our remnant, and to keep destruction and the plague from us and from all his people, the house of Israel; and let us say, Amen.' Morning Service.[3]

### (5) *Give us this day our daily bread*

'Rabbi Joshua said, So that a man should gather on the day for the morrow, as on a sabbath eve for sabbath. Rabbi Eleazar ha-Modai said, So that a man should not gather on the day for the morrow, as on a sabbath eve for sabbath, for it is said, " the thing of the day in its day." He who created the day created its provision. Hence Rabbi Eleazar ha-Modai said, Whosoever has what to eat to-day, and says, What shall I eat to-morrow? lo! such an one is wanting in faith, for it is said, "That I may prove him, whether he will walk in my law, or not." Rabbi Eleazar of Modin, c. A.D. 50–135.[4]

[1] Yoma, 39*a*.     [2] Singer, p. 69.     [3] *Ibid.*
[4] Mechilta on Exod. xvi. 4; *cf.* Sotah, 48b.

# Illustrations from Jewish Sources

'Bless this year unto us, O Lord our God, together with every kind of the produce thereof, for our welfare; give a blessing upon the face of the earth.' From the Eighteen Benedictions.[1]

'Blessed art thou, O Lord our God, King of the universe, who bringest forth bread from the earth.' Grace before Meals, Blessing pronounced over the Bread.[2]

'Blessed art thou, O Lord our God, King of the universe, who feedest the whole world with thy goodness, with grace, with lovingkindness and tender mercy; thou givest food to all flesh, for thy lovingkindness endureth for ever. Through thy great goodness food hath never failed us: O may it not fail us for ever and ever for thy great name's sake, since thou nourishest and sustainest all beings, and doest good unto all, and providest food for all thy creatures whom thou hast created. Blessed art thou, O Lord, who givest food unto all.' Grace after Meals.[3]

*(6) And forgive us our debts, as we also have forgiven our debtors*

'All is given on pledge, and the net is spread over all the living; and the shop is open and the shopman gives credit, and the account-book is open and the hand writes, and every

---

[1] Singer, p. 47.   [2] *Ibid.* p. 278.   [3] *Ibid.* p. 286.

# The Lord's Prayer

one who will borrow comes and borrows, and the collectors go round continually every day, and exact payment from man whether with his knowledge or without it; and they have whereon to lean, and the judgment is a judgment of truth; and everything is prepared for the banquet.' Rabbi Akiba, A.D. 50–135.[1]

'All who are forbearing and forgiving and do not insist on their rights will be forgiven.'[2]

'For certain sins repentance gives a respite, and the Day of Atonement atones; but he who sins against his neighbour must first be reconciled to him.'[3]

'So long as we are merciful, God is merciful; but if we are not merciful to others, God is not merciful to us.'[4]

'May it be thy will . . . that hatred of us may not come into the heart of man, nor hatred of man come into our heart; and that envy of us may not come into the heart of man, nor envy of man come into our heart.'[5]

'Forgive us, O Father, for we have sinned. Pardon us, our King, for we have transgressed.' Eighteen Benedictions.[6]

'Our Father, our King! forgive and pardon all our iniquities.

'Our Father, our King! blot out all our

---

[1] Pirke Aboth, iii. 20.   [2] Yoma, 23a.   [3] Ibid. 85b.
[4] Rosh ha-Shanah, 17a;  cf. Megillah, 28a.
[5] Berakoth (T. J.), 7d.          [6] Singer, p. 46.

# Illustrations from Jewish Sources

transgressions and make them pass away from before thine eyes.

'Our Father, our King! erase in thine abundant mercies all the records of our guilt.

'Our Father, our King! bring us back in perfect repentance unto thee.' Abinu Prayer.[1]

## (7) *And bring us not into temptation, but deliver us from evil*

'Never should a man bring himself into the hands of temptation; for behold David, King of Israel, brought himself into the hands of temptation, and stumbled, when he said, "Examine me, O Lord, and prove me."'[2]

'May it be pleasing in thy sight, O Lord my God and the God of my fathers, that thou wilt deliver me this day and every day from the shameless and from shamelessness, from the evil man, from the evil companion, from the evil neighbour, from evil chance, and from Satan the destroyer; from stern judgment and from the implacable adversary, whether he be a son of the covenant or no.'[3]

'May it be thy will, O Lord my God and the God of my Fathers, that thou wilt break and take away the yoke of the evil inclination from our hearts. For thou didst create us to

---

[1] Singer, p. 56.     [2] Sanhedrin, 107a.
[3] Berakoth, 16b.

# The Lord's Prayer

do thy will, and we are bound to do thy will. Thou desirest, and we desire it. And who hinders us? The leaven in the dough. It is revealed and known before thee, that there is no strength in us to withstand it. But may it please thee, O Lord my God and the God of my fathers, that thou wilt cause it to pass away from us, and that thou wilt subdue it; and we will make thy will our will, with a perfect heart.'[1]

'And may it be thy will, O Lord our God and God of our fathers, to make us familiar with thy Law, and to make us cleave to thy commandments. O lead us not into the power of sin, or of transgression, or of iniquity, or of temptation, or of scorn: let not the evil inclination have sway over us: keep us far from a bad man and a bad companion: make us cleave to the good inclination and to good works: subdue our inclination so that it may submit itself unto thee.' Morning Service.[2]

[1] Berakoth, 17a.   [2] Singer, p. 7.

## CHAPTER XIV

# Versions of the Lord's Prayer

**THE LORD'S PRAYER** *in* The Gospel according to St. Matthew. (*Westcott and Hort.*)

Πάτερ ἡμῶν ὁ ἐν τοῖς οὐρανοῖς·
Ἁγιασθήτω τὸ ὄνομά σου,
ἐλθέτω ἡ βασιλεία σου,
γενηθήτω τὸ θέλημά σου,
ὡς ἐν οὐρανῷ καὶ ἐπὶ γῆς·
Τὸν ἄρτον ἡμῶν τὸν ἐπιούσιον
δὸς ἡμῖν σήμερον·
Καὶ ἄφες ἡμῖν τὰ ὀφειλήματα ἡμῶν,
ὡς καὶ ἡμεῖς ἀφήκαμεν τοῖς ὀφειλέταις ἡμῶν·
Καὶ μὴ εἰσενέγκῃς ἡμᾶς εἰς πειρασμόν,
ἀλλὰ ῥῦσαι ἡμᾶς ἀπὸ τοῦ πονηροῦ.

**THE LORD'S PRAYER** *in* The Gospel according to St. Luke. (*Westcott and Hort.*)

Πάτερ, ἁγιασθήτω τὸ ὄνομά σου· ἐλθέτω ἡ βασιλεία σου· τὸν ἄρτον ἡμῶν τὸν ἐπιούσιον δίδου ἡμῖν τὸ καθ' ἡμέραν· καὶ ἄφες ἡμῖν τὰς ἁμαρτίας ἡμῶν, καὶ γὰρ αὐτοὶ ἀφίομεν παντὶ ὀφείλοντι ἡμῖν· καὶ μὴ εἰσενέγκῃς ἡμᾶς εἰς πειρασμόν.

# The Lord's Prayer

**THE LORD'S PRAYER** *in* The Gospel according to St. Matthew. (*Revised Version.*)

Our Father which art in heaven, Hallowed be thy name. Thy kingdom come. Thy will be done, as in heaven, so on earth. Give us this day [1] our daily bread. And forgive us our debts, as we also have forgiven our debtors. And bring us not into temptation, but deliver us from [2] the evil *one*.

**THE LORD'S PRAYER** *in* The Gospel according to St. Luke. (*Revised Version.*)

Father, Hallowed be thy name. Thy kingdom come. Give us day by day [3] our daily bread. And forgive us our sins; for we ourselves also forgive every one that is indebted to us. And bring us not into temptation.

**THE LORD'S PRAYER** *in* The Gospel according to St. Matthew. (*Vulgate.*)

Pater noster qui es in caelis, sanctificetur nomen tuum: adueniat regnum tuum: fiat

---

[1] Margin, Gr. *our bread for the coming day.*
[2] Do. Or, *evil.*
[3] Do. Gr. *our bread for the coming day.*

# Versions of the Lord's Prayer

uoluntas tua sicut in caelo et in terra. Panem nostrum supersubstantialem da nobis hodie: et dimitte nobis debita nostra, sicut et nos dimittimus debitoribus nostris: et ne inducas nos in temtationem: sed libera nos a malo.

### THE LORD'S PRAYER *in* The Gospel according to St. Luke. (*Vulgate*.)

Pater, sanctificetur nomen tuum: adueniat regnum tuum. Panem nostrum cotidianum da nobis cotidie: et dimitte nobis peccata nostra, siquidem et ipsi dimittimus omni debenti nobis: et ne nos inducas in temtationem.

### THE LORD'S PRAYER *in* The Book of Common Prayer. (*With doxology*.)

Our Father, which art in heaven, Hallowed be thy Name. Thy kingdom come. Thy will be done, in earth as it is in heaven. Give us this day our daily bread. And forgive us our trespasses, As we forgive them that trespass against us. And lead us not into temptation; But deliver us from evil: For thine is the kingdom, The power, and the glory, For ever and ever. Amen.

# The Lord's Prayer

## THE LORD'S PRAYER *in* The Teaching of the Twelve Apostles.

Πάτερ ἡμῶν ὁ ἐν τῷ οὐρανῷ, ἁγιασθήτω τὸ ὄνομά σου, ἐλθέτω ἡ βασιλεία σου, γενηθήτω τὸ θέλημά σου ὡς ἐν οὐρανῷ καὶ ἐπὶ γῆς· τὸν ἄρτον ἡμῶν τὸν ἐπιούσιον δὸς ἡμῖν σήμερον, καὶ ἄφες ἡμῖν τὴν ὀφειλὴν ἡμῶν ὡς καὶ ἡμεῖς ἀφίεμεν τοῖς ὀφειλέταις ἡμῶν, καὶ μὴ εἰσενέγκῃς ἡμᾶς εἰς πειρασμόν, ἀλλὰ ῥῦσαι ἡμᾶς ἀπὸ τοῦ πονηροῦ· ὅτι σοῦ ἐστὶν ἡ δύναμις καὶ ἡ δόξα εἰς τοὺς αἰῶνας.

## THE LORD'S PRAYER in St. Cyprian (*De Oratione Dominica*).

Pater noster, qui es in caelis, sanctificetur nomen tuum: adueniat regnum tuum: fiat uoluntas tua sicut in caelo et in terra. Panem nostrum cotidianum da nobis hodie; et remitte nobis debita nostra, sicut et nos remittimus debitoribus nostris: et ne nos patiaris induci in temtationem, sed libera nos a malo.

CHAPTER XV

## THE PRAYERS OF OUR LORD *in* The Synoptic Gospels.

| St. Matthew xi. 25–26 | St. Luke x. 21. |
|---|---|
| At that season Jesus answered and said, I [1] thank thee, O Father, Lord of heaven and earth, that thou didst hide these things from the wise and understanding, and didst reveal them unto babes: yea, Father, [2] for so it was well-pleasing in thy sight. | In that same hour he rejoiced [3] in the Holy Spirit, and said, I [1] thank thee, O Father, Lord of heaven and earth, that thou didst hide these things from the wise and understanding, and didst reveal them unto babes: yea, Father; [2] for so it was well-pleasing in thy sight. |

St. Luke xxii. 31–32.—Simon, Simon, behold, Satan asked to have you, that he might sift you as wheat: but I made supplication for thee, that thy faith fail not.

[1] Margin, Or, *praise.*
[2] Do. Or, *that.*
[3] Do. Or, *by.*

# The Lord's Prayer

| St. Mark xiv. 35–36, 39. | St. Matthew xxvi. 39, 42. | St. Luke xxii. 42. |
|---|---|---|
| Abba, Father, all things are possible unto thee; remove this cup from me: howbeit not what I will, but what thou wilt.... And again he went away, and prayed, and spake the same words. | O my Father, if it be possible, let this cup pass away from me: nevertheless not as I will, but as thou wilt.... Again a second time he went away, and prayed, saying, O my Father, if this cannot pass away, except I drink it, thy will be done. | Father, if thou be willing, remove this cup from me: nevertheless not my will, but thine, be done. |

St. Luke xxiii. 34.—Father, forgive them, for they know not what they do.

St. Luke xxiii. 46.—Father, into thy hands I commend my spirit.

# The Prayers of our Lord

**THE PRAYERS OF OUR LORD** *in* The Fourth Gospel.

### St. John xi. 41-42.

And Jesus lifted up his eyes, and said, Father, I thank thee that thou heardest me. And I knew that thou hearest me always : but because of the multitude which standeth around I said it, that they may believe that thou didst send me.

### St. John xii. 27-28.

Now is my soul troubled ; and what shall I say ? Father, save me from this hour. But for this cause came I unto this hour. Father, glorify thy name.

### St. John xvii.

These things spake Jesus ; and lifting up his eyes to heaven, he said, Father, the hour is come ; glorify thy Son, that the Son may glorify thee : even as thou gavest him authority over all flesh, that whatsoever thou hast given him, to them he should give eternal life. And this is life eternal, that they should know thee the only true God, and him whom thou didst send, *even* Jesus Christ. I glorified thee on the earth, having accomplished the work which thou hast given me to do. And now, O Father,

# The Lord's Prayer

glorify thou me with thine own self with the glory which I had with thee before the world was. I manifested thy name unto the men whom thou gavest me out of the world: thine they were, and thou gavest them to me; and they have kept thy word. Now they know that all things whatsoever thou hast given me are from thee: for the words which thou gavest me I have given unto them; and they received *them*, and knew of a truth that I came forth from thee, and they believed that thou didst send me. I pray for them: I pray not for the world, but for those whom thou hast given me; for they are thine: and all things that are mine are thine, and thine are mine: and I am glorified in them. And I am no more in the world, and these are in the world, and I come to thee. Holy Father, keep them in thy name which thou hast given me, that they may be one, even as we *are*. While I was with them, I kept them in thy name which thou hast given me: and I guarded them, and not one of them perished, but the son of perdition; that the scripture might be fulfilled. But now I come to thee; and these things I speak in the world, that they may have my joy fulfilled in themselves. I have given them thy word; and the world hated them, because they are not of the world, even as I am not of the world. I pray not that thou shouldest

# The Prayers of our Lord

take them from the world, but that thou shouldest keep them from the evil¹ *one*. They are not of the world, even as I am not of the world. Sanctify them in the truth: thy word is truth. As thou didst send me into the world, even so sent I them into the world. And for their sakes I sanctify myself, that they themselves also may be sanctified in truth. Neither for these only do I pray, but for them also that believe on me through their word; that they may all be one; even as thou, Father, *art* in me, and I in thee, that they also may be in us: that the world may believe that thou didst send me. And the glory which thou hast given me I have given unto them; that they may be one, even as we *are* one; I in them, and thou in me, that they may be perfected into one; that the world may know that thou didst send me, and lovedst them, even as thou lovedst me. Father, that which thou hast given me, I will that, where I am, they also may be with me; that they may behold my glory, which thou hast given me: for thou lovedst me before the foundation of the world. O righteous Father, the world knew thee not, but I knew thee; and these knew that thou didst send me; and I made known unto them thy name, and will make it known; that the love wherewith thou lovedst me may be in them, and I in them.

# Index of References

### GENESIS
| | PAGE |
|---|---|
| XIV. 19 ff | 33 |
| XV. 2 | 15 |
| XXII. 1 | 125 |

### EXODUS
| | |
|---|---|
| XVI. 4 | 99, 100 |
| XVI. 13 f | 101 |
| XVI. 15 ff | 100 |
| XVII. 7 | 130 |
| XX. 7 | 39 |
| XXIII. 4 f | 116 |
| XXXII. 27 | 40 |

### LEVITICUS
| | |
|---|---|
| XI. 45 | 46 |
| XXIV. 11 | 39 |

### NUMBERS
| | |
|---|---|
| XII. 3 | 58 |

### DEUTERONOMY
| | |
|---|---|
| VII. 21 | 15 |
| VIII. 3 | 94 |
| XII. 11 | 39 |
| XV. 1 f. | 117 |

### 2 SAMUEL
| | |
|---|---|
| VII. 14 | 14 |
| VII. 27 | 15 |

### 1 KINGS
| | PAGE |
|---|---|
| VIII. 25 | 15 |
| XVIII. 26 | 8 |

### 2 KINGS
| | |
|---|---|
| IX. 11 | 58 |

### 1 CHRONICLES
| | |
|---|---|
| XXIX. 10 f. | 138 |
| XXIX. 13 | 140 |
| XXIX. 20 | 139 |

### 2 CHRONICLES
| | |
|---|---|
| VI. 21 | 111 |
| VI. 29 | 111 |

### EZRA
| | |
|---|---|
| VIII. 31 | 125 |

### NEHEMIAH
| | |
|---|---|
| I. 4 | 33 |
| I. 5 | 15 |
| VIII. 6 | 140 |
| IX. 32 | 15 |

### JOB
| | |
|---|---|
| XIII. 14 f | 84 |

### PSALMS
| | |
|---|---|
| IX. 10 | 38 |
| XVII. 7 | 15 |
| XXIII. 5 | 94 |

### PSALMS
| | PAGE |
|---|---|
| XXVIII. 1 | 16 |
| XL. 8 | 81, 147 |
| LXVII. 2 | 40 |
| LXVIII. 5 | 14 |
| LXXIII. 25 | 34 |
| LXXVIII. 19 | 94 |
| LXXX. 1 | 16 |
| LXXXVIII. 1 | 16 |
| XCIX. 3 | 40 |
| CIII. 13 | 14 |
| CXV. 1 | 137 |
| CXV. 2 f | 138 |
| CXXVI. 3 | 137 |
| CXLV. 18 | 35 |
| CXLVI. 6 | 33 |

### PROVERBS
| | |
|---|---|
| IX. 10 | 37 |
| XXIV. 17 | 116 |
| XXV. 21 | 116 |
| XXX. 8 f | 98 |

### ECCLESIASTES
| | |
|---|---|
| V. 2 | 34 |

### ISAIAH
| | |
|---|---|
| VI. 1 | 35 |
| IX. 6 f | 80 |
| XI. 2 | 80 |
| XI. 9 | 52 |
| XXXII. 1 | 49 |

# Index of References

## ISAIAH

| | PAGE |
|---|---|
| LI. 13. | 33 |
| LV. 9. | 35 |
| LVII. 15 | 34 |
| LXI. 2 | 117 |
| LXIII. 8 | 15 |
| LXIII. 16 | 13, 15 |
| LXIV. 8 | 15 |

## JEREMIAH

| | |
|---|---|
| XIV. 8 | 15 |
| XXIX. 13 | 1 |

## EZEKIEL

| | |
|---|---|
| XXXVI. 23 | 39 |

## DANIEL

| | |
|---|---|
| II. 19. | 33 |
| II. 44 | 48 |
| VII. 27 | 49 |
| IX. 4. | 15 |
| XI. 32 | 49 |

## HOSEA

| | |
|---|---|
| XI. 1. | 13 |
| XI. 4. | 50 |

## JOEL

| | |
|---|---|
| II. 28 ff | 68 |

## HABAKKUK

| | |
|---|---|
| II. 14. | 52 |

## ZECHARIAH

| | |
|---|---|
| XIV. 9 | 46, 48 |

## MALACHI

| | PAGE |
|---|---|
| II. 10. | 14 |
| IV. 2. | 37 |

## TOBIT

| | |
|---|---|
| XII. 8 | 16 |
| XIII. 4 | 17 |

## WISDOM

| | |
|---|---|
| II. 16. | 17 |
| V. 5. | 17 |
| XIV. 3 | 16 |
| XVI. 13 f | 101 |
| XVI. 28 | 16 |

## ECCLESIASTICUS

| | |
|---|---|
| XXIII. 1 | 16 |
| XXVIII. 2 | 117 |

## MATTHEW

| | |
|---|---|
| II. 2. | 91 |
| IV. 4. | 130 |
| IV. 8. | 72 |
| IV. 17 | 57, 91 |
| IV. 23 | 50 |
| V. 6. | 55, 147 |
| V. 11. | 57 |
| V. 16. | 20, 43 |
| V. 17. | 5 |
| V. 20. | 80 |
| V. 44. | 24 |
| V. 45. | 20 |
| V. 48. | 20, 46 |
| VI. 5 ff | 3 |
| VI. 7. | 8 |

## MATTHEW

| | PAGE |
|---|---|
| VI. 9. | 5, 28 |
| VI. 10 | 33, 48 |
| VI. 12 | 109 |
| VI. 13 | 123 |
| VI. 22 | 81 |
| VI. 26 | 21 |
| VI. 32 | 34, 92 |
| VI. 33 | 60, 70, 94, 147 |
| VI. 34 | 98, 130 |
| VII. 7 | 56 |
| VII. 11 | 19, 116, 153 |
| VII. 21 | 80, 148 |
| VIII. 11 | 130 |
| VIII. 20 | 88 |
| IX. 2. | 121 |
| IX. 37 | 53 |
| X. 22 | 64 |
| XI. 5. | 52, 92 |
| XI. 12 | 54 |
| XI. 25 | 32, 59, 153 |
| XI. 25 ff | 12, 23, 73 |
| XI. 26 | 138, 150 |
| XI. 27 | 74 |
| XII. 35 | 134 |
| XIII. 11 | 70 |
| XIII. 19 | 155 |
| XIII. 21 | 157 |
| XIII. 22 | 96, 130 |
| XIII. 29 | 164 |
| XIII. 38 | 122 |
| XIII. 43 | 39, 71 |
| XIII. 46 | 55 |
| XIII. 52 | 82 |
| XIV. 19 | 33 |
| XV. 19 | 134 |
| XVI. 4 | 131 |

# Index of References

| MATTHEW | | |
|---|---|---|
| | | PAGE |
| XVIII. 3 | 22, 59, 73 | |
| XVIII. 10 ff. | | 164 |
| XVIII. 14 | 81, 148 | |
| XVIII. 17 | . | 162 |
| XVIII. 31 | . | 162 |
| XIX. 1 | . | 161 |
| XX. 9 | . | 107 |
| XXI. 31 | . | 114 |
| XXII. 4 | . | 53 |
| XXIII. 9 | 21, 35 | |
| XXIII. 34 | . | 82 |
| XXIV. 3 | 57, 62 | |
| | | 132 |
| XXIV. 6 | . | 62 |
| XXIV. 10 | . | 132 |
| XXIV. 13 | . | 132 |
| XXIV. 14 | . | 167 |
| XXIV. 34 | . | 62 |
| XXIV. 43 | | 170 |
| XXIV. 45 ff | | 164 |
| XXIV. 46 | . | 65 |
| XXIV. 48 | . | 61 |
| XXV. 21 | 65, 85, 86 | |
| XXV. 40 | . | 59 |
| XXVI. 11 | . | 92 |
| XXVI. 41 | . | 126 |
| XXVI. 42 | . 23, 29 | |
| XXVIII. 19 | . | 166 |

| MARK | | |
|---|---|---|
| I. 15 | . | 50 |
| II. 14 | . | 58 |
| III. 31 ff | . | 131 |
| IV. 11 | . | 59 |
| IV. 15 | . | 155 |
| IV. 28 | . | 60 |
| VI. 21 | . | 97 |
| VI. 41 | 33, 105 | |
| VII. 27 | . | 108 |
| VII. 34 | . | 33 |
| VII. 36 | . | 131 |
| VIII. 11 | . | 130 |
| VIII. 14 | . | 93 |
| VIII. 33 | . | 131 |
| VIII. 35 | . | 66 |
| IX. 1 | . | 56 |
| IX. 43 ff | . | 67 |
| X. 23 | . | 97 |
| X. 29 | . | 66 |
| X. 38 | . | 60 |
| X. 45 | . | 61 |
| XI. 24 f | . | 3 |
| XI. 25 | 36, 115 | |
| XIII. 32 | 62, 63 | |
| XIII. 33 | 63, 64 | |
| XIII. 36 | . | 63 |
| XIV. 34 | . | 132 |
| XIV. 36 | 23, 29, | |
| | 35, 89, 144 | |
| XIV. 37 | . | 129 |
| XIV. 38 | . | 129 |
| XV. 34 | . | 24 |

| LUKE | | |
|---|---|---|
| I. 75 | . | 146 |
| II. 14 | 79, 138, 150 | |
| IV. 14 | . | 153 |
| IV. 18 | . | 152 |
| IV. 19 | . | 117 |
| VI. 5 | . | 52 |
| VI. 21 | . | 147 |
| VI. 27 f | . | 119 |
| VI. 46 | . | 148 |
| VII. 37 ff | . | 113 |
| VII. 47 | . | 113 |
| VIII. 12 | . | 155 |

| LUKE | | |
|---|---|---|
| | | PAGE |
| VIII. 13 | . | 126 |
| IX. 16 | . | 33 |
| IX. 62 | . | 55 |
| X. 21 | 23, 73, 138, | |
| | | 150 |
| X. 21 f | 12, 153 | |
| X. 22 | . | 74 |
| XI. 1 | . | 28 |
| XI. 1 f | | 9 |
| XI. 2 | . | 3, 28 |
| XI. 4 | . | 115 |
| XI. 9 | . | 56 |
| XI. 13 | . | 153 |
| XI. 20 | . | 52 |
| XI. 28 | . | 148 |
| XII. 19 | . | 78 |
| XII. 31 | . | 147 |
| XII. 32 | 55, 71, 73, | |
| | | 150 |
| XII. 49 | . | 53 |
| XII. 51 | . | 67 |
| XIV. 15 ff | . | 104 |
| XIV. 28 | . | 60 |
| XIV. 31 | 60, 125 | |
| XV. 2 | . | 104 |
| XV. 3 ff | . | 164 |
| XV. 7 | . | 148 |
| XV. 17 | . | 22 |
| XV. 18 | . | 21 |
| XV. 19 | . | 112 |
| XV. 21 | . | 112 |
| XVI. 16 | . | 55 |
| XVII. 3 f | . | 119 |
| XVII. 20 | . | 64 |
| XVII. 21 | 60, 63, 72 | |
| XVII. 22 | . | 54 |
| XVIII. 8 | . | 65 |
| XVIII. 11 | . | 81 |

# Index of References

## LUKE

| | PAGE |
|---|---|
| XIX. 10 | 52 |
| XIX. 17 | 86 |
| XXI. 5 | 157 |
| XXI. 18 f | 157 |
| XXII. 28 f | 71 |
| XXII. 28-34 | 128 |
| XXII. 42 | 23, 29, 72, 144 |
| XXII. 58 | 130 |
| XXIII. 34 | 120 |
| XXIII. 46 | 24 |

## JOHN

| | PAGE |
|---|---|
| I. 12 | 41 |
| II. 17 | 53 |
| III. 8 | 69 |
| IV. 34 | 88 |
| IV. 36 | 63 |
| V. 17 | 79 |
| VI. 15 | 131 |
| VI. 32 | 103 |
| VI. 35 | 103 |
| VI. 38 | 87 |
| VI. 41 | 103 |
| VI. 68 | 66 |
| VII. 17 | 78, 87 |
| VIII. 7 | 114 |
| IX. 2 ff | 88 |
| IX. 4 | 54, 57 |
| IX. 31 | 147 |
| XI. 9 | 54 |
| XI. 41 | 32 |
| XI. 41 f | 26 |
| XII. 25 | 67 |
| XII. 27 | 26 |
| XII. 27 f | 127 |
| XII. 28 | 25 f, 33, 37, 44 |

## JOHN

| | PAGE |
|---|---|
| XII. 28 ff | 89 |
| XII. 30 | 26 |
| XII. 32 | 70 |
| XIII. 31 | 44 |
| XIII. 34 f | 81 |
| XIV. 12 | 69 |
| XIV. 27 | 69 |
| XV. 12 f | 67 |
| XV. 13 | 86 |
| XV. 26 | 69 |
| XVI. 13 | 69 |
| XVI. 27 | 19, 34 |
| XVI. 33 | 68 |
| XVII. 1 | 25, 32, 34, 45 |
| XVII. 2 | 74 |
| XVII. 3 | 70 |
| XVII. 4 | 45, 74 |
| XVII. 5 | 25 |
| XVII. 6 | 11, 42, 47 |
| XVII. 11 | 25, 42, 45, 47, 75 |
| XVII. 12 | 42, 47 |
| XVII. 13 | 27 |
| xvii. 15 | 127 |
| XVII. 17 | 43 |
| XVII. 19 | 43 |
| XVII. 20 f | 75 |
| XVII. 21 | 25 |
| XVII. 22 | 45 |
| XVII. 22 ff | 75 |
| XVII. 25 f | 45 |
| XVII. 26 | 42 |
| XVIII. 33 | 71 |
| XVIII. 36 | 71 |
| XXI. 22 f | 162 |
| XXI. 23 | 65 |

## ACTS

| | PAGE |
|---|---|
| I. 7 | 63 |
| I. 8 | 69 |
| IV. 13 | 53 |
| IX. 6 | 86 |
| X. 38 | 69 |
| XIV. 17 | 40 |
| XXII. 12, 14 | 149 |

## ROMANS

| | |
|---|---|
| II. 18 | 147 |
| VI. 1 | 113 |
| VI. 22 | 113 |
| VIII. 15 | 11, 18 |
| VIII. 26 | 85 |
| IX. 4 | 18 |
| XII. 21 | 123 |
| XIV. 7 | 105 |
| XV. 3 | 87 |

## 1 CORINTHIANS

| | |
|---|---|
| I. 25 | 23 |
| III. 9 | 76, 79, 90 |
| VII. 29 | 56, 84, 161 |
| X. 16 | 105 |
| XIII. 5 | 118 |
| XV. 28 | 75 |
| XV. 54 | 87 |
| XV. 57 | 137 |

## 2 CORINTHIANS

| | |
|---|---|
| VIII. 9 | 92 |
| XII. 7 | 84 |
| XII. 9 | 84 |

## GALATIANS

| | |
|---|---|
| II. 4 | 146 |
| II. 21 | 146 |

# Index of References

## GALATIANS
| | PAGE |
|---|---|
| III. 2 | 146 |
| VI. 2 | 96 |

## EPHESIANS
| | PAGE |
|---|---|
| I. 9 | 76, 90 |
| IV. 6 | 28 |
| IV. 25 | 111 |
| IV. 32 | 122 |
| V. 15 ff | 82 |

## PHILIPPIANS
| | PAGE |
|---|---|
| I. 27 | 54 |
| IV. 6 | 107 |

## COLOSSIANS
| | PAGE |
|---|---|
| IV. 11 | 48 |

## 2 THESSALONIANS
| | PAGE |
|---|---|
| III. 10 | 96 |

## 1 TIMOTHY
| | PAGE |
|---|---|
| VI. 12 | 57 |

## 2 TIMOTHY
| | PAGE |
|---|---|
| IV. 17 ff | 156 |

## HEBREWS
| | PAGE |
|---|---|
| II. 10 | 44 |
| II. 17 f | 125 |
| IV. 15 | 120, 126 |
| V. 7 | 24, 150 |
| X. 22 | 35 |
| XII. 1 f | 111 |
| XII. 22 | 35 |

## JAMES
| | PAGE |
|---|---|
| I. 2 ff | 125 |
| I. 13 | 123 |

## 1 PETER
| | PAGE |
|---|---|
| I. 6 | 133 |
| III. 8 | 109, 113 |
| IV. 7 | 132 |
| V. 8 | 133, 156 |

## 1 JOHN
| | PAGE |
|---|---|
| I. 8 | 111 |
| I. 10 | 111 |
| III. 14 ff | 65 |
| III. 20 | 112 |
| V. 4 | 68 |
| V. 14 | 77, 145 |

## REVELATION
| | PAGE |
|---|---|
| II. 4 | 70 |
| II. 13 | 133, 155 |
| II. 17 | 40, 42, 54 |
| III. 3 | 64 |
| III. 10 | 133 |
| VI. 10 | 62 |
| XV. 4 | 38 |

## PSEUDEPIGRAPHA

### Jubilees
| | PAGE |
|---|---|
| I. 25 | 17 |

### Story of Ahikar
| | PAGE |
|---|---|
| II. 20 | 118 |

### Test. Gad.
| | PAGE |
|---|---|
| VI. 3-7 | 118 |

### Test. Zeb.
| | PAGE |
|---|---|
| VIII. 5 | 118 |

## MISHNA

### Berakoth
| | PAGE |
|---|---|
| IV. 3 | 4 |

### Pirke Aboth
| | PAGE |
|---|---|
| II. 16 | 172 |
| III. 20 | 178 |
| IV. 2 | 175 |
| IV. 5 | 172 |
| V. 23 | 34 |

### Rosh-ha-Shana
| | PAGE |
|---|---|
| III. 8 | 171 |

### Sotah
| | PAGE |
|---|---|
| IX. 11 | 171 |

### Yoma
| | PAGE |
|---|---|
| VIII. 9 | 171 |

## BABYLONIAN TALMUD

### Berakoth
| | PAGE |
|---|---|
| 16b | 175, 179 |
| 17a | 175, 180 |
| 29b | 175 |
| 40b | 42, 172, 174 |

# Index of References

| Megillah | PAGE |
|---|---|
| 28a | 178 |

| Rosh ha-Shanah | PAGE |
|---|---|
| 17a | 178 |

| Sanhedrin | PAGE |
|---|---|
| 107a | 179 |

| Sotah | PAGE |
|---|---|
| 48b | 176 |

| Yoma | PAGE |
|---|---|
| 39a | 176 |

### JERUSALEM TALMUD

| Berakoth | PAGE |
|---|---|
| 7d | 178 |

| Mechilta | PAGE |
|---|---|
| 56a | 174, 176 |

| Siphra | PAGE |
|---|---|
| 93d | 171 |

| Siphri | PAGE |
|---|---|
| 87² | 175 |

| Seder Rab Amram | |
|---|---|
| I. 3b | 173 f |
| I. 9b | 173 |
| I. 10b | 174 |

| Wayyikra Rabbah | |
|---|---|
| 32 | 175 |

# General Index

ABBA, 23, 29, 143
Abbott, E. A., 31, 101
Akiba, Rabbi, 4
Angels, 79, 138, 150
Apocalyptic, 49, 51
Asceticism, 161 ff
Athlete, Christian, 54, 84, 86
Atonement, 121 f
Augustine, St., 123, 134
Authorship of Lord's Prayer, 6–8

BAAL, prophets of, 8
Baptism, 166
Basil, St., 108
Beatitudes, 57
Benedictions, Jewish, 42, 138 f
Bernard, J. H., 121
Bilingual prayer, 30
Book of Common Prayer, 80, 85, 134
Browning, R., 79
Bunyan, 54
Butler, Bishop, 51

CHARITY, 107 f.
Chase, F. H., 36, 98, 139
Chasidim, 7
Clement, St., 107

DANTE, 54, 90
Decalogue, 39
Deissmann, 167

Deliberation, 60, 125 f
Denney, J., 94
Devil, 134–6
Didache, 139, 165, 184
Dualism, 67, 124

ECONOMICS, 94 f
Eighteen Benedictions, 4
Endeavour, Gospel of, 52, 86, 111
Environment, 121
Eschatology, 56 f, 62–7, 155, 169 f
Ethics, 21, 59, 76, 80, 160 f
Eucharist, 104–6, 140, 164 f

FAILURE, 110 f
Faith, 64 f
Family prayer, 21, 41, 74, 136
Father as title of God in Old Testament, 13, 16
Father as title of God in Apocrypha, 16 f
Father as title of God in Gospels, 18–27
Father as title of God in Talmud, 17 f, 33 f, 143
Forgiveness, in Old Testament, 116 f
Forgiveness in Apocrypha, 117 f
Forgiveness in Gospels, 114 f, 118 f

# General Index

Forgiveness in pagan ethics, 116
Fountain prayers, 4

GETHSEMANE, 23, 72, 89 f, 126, 150
Gore, Bishop, 35, 106

HEREDITY, 121
Holy Spirit, 68–70, 151–3
Hope, Gospel of, 52

LAST Supper, 25, 105
Latimer, Bishop, 5
Legalism, 81, 145–9
Liturgical usage, 28, 30, 97

MANICHÆAN, 135
Manna, 99–103
Massah, 130
Maurice, F. D., 30
Messianic meal, 93 f, 104
Missionary prayer, 46, 145–58

OCCASION of Lord's Prayer, 8–10, 142
Odes of Solomon, 168 f
Origen, 31, 106
Other-worldliness, 61

PAROUSIA, 68, 159–170
Paternoster, 22, 51
Persecution, 132–4, 155–8
Petitionary prayer, 107

Pilate, 71, 156
Plato, 81
Poverty, 92 f, 95
Prayers, Gentile, 8
Prayers, Jewish, 3 f, 17 f
Prodigal Son, 21, 112

REPENTANCE, 110 f, 114, 119
Resignation, 75, 82 f
Robinson, J. A., 9

SABBATH, 52
Selfishness, 131 f, 136
Service, 61
Shaw, G. B., 58
Sin, 110–14
Singer, Jewish Prayer Book, 39, 139, 172–80
Son of Man, 20, 52
Sovereignty of God, 8 f, 51
Suffering, 83–5, 88 f, 92
Superman, 58

TALMUDIC quotations, 6 f
Temptation of Our Lord, 50, 72, 102, 105, 127, 130–2
Theocracy, 51

UNDERSTANDING, prayer as, 81, 85 f, 120

WAR, 57, 86 f, 120
Wealth, 96 f

www.ingramcontent.com/pod-product-compliance
Lightning Source LLC
Chambersburg PA
CBHW072127160426
43197CB00012B/2018